To the spirit that lives in all of us,
with a prayer that we will remember our oneness

And did you get what you wanted from this life, even so?
I did.
And what did you want?
To call myself beloved, to feel myself beloved on the earth.
—RAYMOND CARVER

Contents

V LOVING

Introduction

My Story

My first spiritual teacher was my mother. As a young girl in Athens, Greece, I remember seeing my mother sitting in our living room, drinking tea and eating her favorite biscuits, in contemplation. It looked like she was doing nothing, but over time I realized this was her time of spiritual communion. In quiet reflection, she seemed to be drawing upon something deep within herself. She was listening for guidance and direction as she orchestrated various aspects of our lives. This was her form of prayer. My mother always trusted that help would come her way, and indeed it did. She made miracles happen for me and my sister, taking us from Athens to London, finding us the best schools and teachers, and making a home for us in a foreign country. Support showed up in countless ways in her life and, therefore, in ours.

I began to realize that she was connected by an invisible lifeline to a greater source, and by following its guidance, she opened unimaginable doors for us. Whenever I was faced with a decision and didn't know what to do, my mother would say *Let it marinate, darling*. She never rushed to solutions. She trusted that spiritual guidance could not be hurried. My mother's wisdom was remarkable to experience and absorb, and I know it allowed her to stay calm and faithful in the face of adversity.

My mother demonstrated every day how to offer and receive at the same time. This instilled in me a belief that something far beyond my physical reality is always present and supporting me. I have drawn on this unshakable source of trust all my life. This belief has also given me permission to be generous with myself, both in giving and receiving, and has allowed me to open myself up to others. I have always found spirituality in connecting with others and that's where I began to discover the power of my spirit, freely giving of my love and feeling a resonance with the world that further opened me up to a sense of oneness.

Aside from weddings, baptisms, funerals, and Easter Sunday, we didn't go to church. My mother used to say, "Our home is our church." On a beautiful table in our front hallway, she set up trays of dried fruit, nuts of every kind, and, of course, wheat—the symbol of abundance. This was her altar. She extended a heartfelt offering to everyone that she met and a warm welcome to everyone who came to our home. Every day, my sister and I would come home from school and sit with our mother in our little kitchen, eating a homemade meal and sharing how our day went. She called this our human communion.

My mother continued to search for deeper spiritual knowledge and was led to yoga and meditation. She introduced me and my sister to yoga when we were teenagers. There we were, in Athens, Greece, without a television, learning the practice of yoga. At the tender age of twelve, the seeds of spirituality were planted in me. She also kept the book *Autobiography of a Yogi* by Paramahansa Yogananda, written in Greek, next to her bed, which became the book that led to my spiritual awakening later in my life.

My father, a brilliant young journalist in Athens, was working on a manifesto for a new vision of Greece during the Second World War. He was arrested by the Nazis and held in a concentration camp for a year and a half. When he shared with us stories about his time in the camps, he told us that every night he lay awake in his cell, editing the manifesto in his mind's eye. This became a lifeline for him, connecting him to the hope and motivation to keep going and giving him faith that he would get out alive and finish the book. This was his form of prayer. He survived, and he always expressed his gratitude to God for surviving. Every night, as he fell asleep, he would cross himself and say *doxasi o theos,* meaning "glory be to God."

Yet my father carried a deep psychic trauma from the suffering of that experience. Over the course of my parents' marriage, he was involved in several extramarital affairs, which caused my mother tremendous pain. Eventually, she left him and raised me and my sister on her own. I always felt her pain, and as I would go to sleep each night, I would pray for my mother to receive help. A soft caress would touch my hand, and I intuitively knew that there was a presence there, looking after me. This was one of my earliest recollections of a connection to that presence, though I did not entirely understand it at the time. I didn't need to understand it in order to believe in it and be comforted by it. I just trusted it, the way I trust that the sun will rise in the morning. But, like many of us, I discounted it as the years went on, and a long time would pass before I remembered it.

If I ask you to remember a time when you felt connected to the presence of "God" or spirit, I am sure you will have a memory of knowing that you are connected to something beyond yourself, something mystical and invisible. When we are children, we live inside of this innate knowing, but as we grow up, we move away from it. We forget. Many of us, at some point, try to remember. For some of us, a recognition lingers. We feel a constant tug or a longing to reconnect with what we know is there. We feel hints of it at different moments: when we watch a glorious sunset, look into a baby's eyes, hear a favorite song or poem, or meet someone who reflects it back to us. We are returned to the inner knowing that a mystical presence is always there.

My spiritual reawakening was a distinct moment. After graduating from drama school in London, I moved to Los Angeles. I had been offered my first acting role and was waiting to hear whether the studio would green-light the movie. It was a very exciting but very uncertain and unpredictable period in my life. I was thrown into this entirely new and unfamiliar world and was far away from my family without any sense of what the outcome would be.

During that time, I was searching for a source of guidance and comfort. I rediscovered yoga and read many spiritual books, including my mother's favorite, *Autobiography of a Yogi*. One night, I was lying in my hotel room, reading the book, and I fell asleep with it open. I had been reading a passage about the yogis who lived for thousands of years, outside of linear time as we know it, traveling beyond their bodies to other realms. It was a very powerful section of the book, which brought me into another dimension of consciousness. I was awakened by the early morning light coming through the window, and I felt a profound inner connection. There was a light within me and all around me. I sensed a presence envelop me, and I fell to my knees, sobbing. I was remembering. It was as if the gates were snapped open, and I was let out of my inner exile. I was not simply a Greek girl named Agapi, alone in Los Angeles, trying to be an actor. I was awakened to the fact that I was far more than my physical body. I felt bathed by this sense of connection; the same presence I had sensed as a young girl in Greece was now palpable in me and all around me. Was it a coincidence or a moment of epiphany? I believe it was grace. I don't think we can will these things to be. I believe that they are given to us. Our souls answer the call. Or maybe we hear the call of our souls, and we answer it.

How ironic that the next day the studio called to tell me the film had fallen through. At the very moment that a door had closed, a new, unknown path was opening before me. I had been given a plane ticket to return to London, but I chose instead to stay in Los Angeles and pursue this deeper spiritual connection, a choice that would allow my destiny to unfold. I remember very clearly asking for a teacher to guide me on this inner journey and that deep request was answered. I was led to my masterful teacher, John-Roger, the founder of the Movement of Spiritual Inner Awareness (MSIA), which is dedicated to a path of soul transcendence. From the moment I first met him, I knew that he was my teacher, and this was my path. With his loving guidance and through his profound teachings, I embarked on a committed, devoted spiritual path that allowed me to discover deeper parts of myself and experience my connection to the inner light, witness its power and its presence, and know its existence in me and in everyone. My journey to soul awareness had begun, and it continues on today.

A World in Crisis

People travel to wonder at the height of the mountains, at the huge waves of the seas, at the long course of the rivers, at the vast compass of the ocean, at the circular motion of the stars, and yet they pass by themselves without wondering.

—St. Augustine

Humanity is in a moment of spiritual crisis. Structured religion, in all its forms, has caused many of us to feel more divided than ever and has alienated us from the truth of our oneness. Over the last three decades, the number of Americans who identify as "none," meaning that they are unaffiliated with any religion, has climbed steadily. Today, as many Americans identify as "not religious" as those who identify as devotees of a particular religion. The decline of organized religion has caused millions of people to feel disconnected from spirituality. Where, then, do people turn for strength and guidance and inspiration? Some look to other sources such as yoga, meditation, astrology, and psychedelic drugs, but in all these efforts, we might be overlooking our innate ability to make direct contact with our inner guidance in every living, breathing moment. Our inner guidance is like a wireless network: it's invisible, but it is available everywhere that we are. We just need to enter the password, and the password is *prayer*.

Imagine for a moment that you are in danger. You're on an airplane that hits a pocket of turbulence, or you're walking down the street and feel the trembling of an earthquake. You are completely vulnerable, at the mercy of your circumstances. Without thinking, you pray.

When we are in crisis, we go to God. We instinctively land there. We turn to prayer when we need a job, when we're faced with a financial challenge, or when we or our loved one is suffering an illness. I am writing this book during the coronavirus pandemic. In a time of tremendous fear, constant uncertainty, and unthinkable loss, people in every corner of the world are turning to prayer. Internet searches for *prayer* skyrocketed as COVID-19 spread. This longing to connect with something larger than ourselves is always in us but is often buried. In times of crisis, it rises to the surface.

What about when you are not in danger, but in a moment of indecision, doubt, hurt, or lack? Where do you turn when you have an idea and aren't sure how to execute it? How about when you want to connect with someone socially or professionally but feel "less than"? Or when you merely feel worried and don't know how to break the cycle of anxious thinking? Anytime you are looking for guidance, for a solution to a problem, or for more vitality and aliveness in your life, start to pray, open yourself to the vast possibilities beyond your own mind, and let your imagination expand and wander. In crisis or not, prayer can bring you back to gratitude; giving thanks for what you have can soften your heart and connect you to your tender spirit. Ultimately, the presence of God is all about unconditional love. When we truly understand this, there is nothing that will stop us from screaming in unbridled joy: *Eureka!*

It takes discipline to turn your attention to prayer, to let go of your worrying. And it takes a sense of worthiness to believe that you are deserving of this awesome connection. So many of us move through our lives feeling unworthy. We believe that in order to claim our power we need to prove our value, but that's the greatest trap of the human condition: we are looking for answers all around us and can't see that the beloved resides within us. So few among us are ever taught this reality. But you can stop exactly where you are in any moment to pray, to call forward the presence here and now.

It's astounding how the quality of your day can completely shift if you are willing to ask for whatever it is you want more of. It is extraordinary how our higher consciousness—the spirit in us—always wants to serve us. But it won't intervene unless we open ourselves to it.

What Is Prayer?

When you really look for me, you will see me instantly—
you will find me in the tiniest house of time,
Kabir says: Student, tell me, what is God?
He is the breath inside the breath.

—KABIR

The Greek word for prayer is *prosefchí,* meaning "toward your wishes." We all want to experience a good life that encompasses health, love, opportunities, and a sense of belonging, and we all have wishes for ourselves and our lives. But our deepest wish is to find meaning and a sense of connection to something larger than ourselves. This is embedded in every human being, even if it isn't conscious. These are the great questions that we each ask: What is the meaning of life? What is the meaning of *my* life? I believe that these fundamental questions can be answered by the power of prayer that connects us to the spirit within, to the God in each of us.

Please don't let the word *God* limit you. *God* can be a loaded word; it means something different to everyone. When I say *God*, I am referring to a transcendent power beyond what words can possibly describe. Connect to the spiritual, cosmic, larger-than-life presence in whatever way resonates with you. Before his events, the poet Mark Nepo often asks his audience if they believe in something larger than themselves. Ninety-nine percent of people raise their hands. "I guess, then," he says, "we are all mystics." Whatever word you want to use, whether it is *God, the light, spirit, the higher self, divine intelligence, the One, the I Am, universal love, a higher power,* or anything else, please use it. It doesn't matter what you call it as long as when you call, you remember that you are calling your maker and calling upon a power that lives in your every cell and in your very own breath. In the prayers that follow, I will address the higher spirit as Beloved because I feel that each soul here on earth is beloved by God, but please substitute any name that resonates with you.

I never think of God as a being; I think of God as a state of being. To enter that state, we have to dare to go beyond our limited sense of ourselves, our minds, our emotions, and our finite perspectives. Prayer is the bridge! I don't know about you, but if I spend one second considering the vastness of our universe, I feel reverence, gratitude, safety, and, ultimately, a sense of awe and joy. I don't presume to know how, but I have a profound feeling that the miraculous energy that created the universe is that which created me. It's a little bit like electricity. When I flip the switch, I trust that the lights will come on. I have no idea how that happens, but I know that it works, and I don't second guess it.

Devoted prayer moves us toward the real connection that we all crave. This is why it is important to put our prayers—our wishes—into words. Words have power, and they carry energy, as do our thoughts. When we pray with intention, blocks can be removed, and the truth can be revealed. When we pray with sincerity and surrender, prayer becomes the gateway to unlocking the higher power, the solutions, and the awareness that we are completely and utterly connected to the unfathomable miracle of life itself. As my teacher John-Roger says, "If you enter into the right consciousness of prayer, you can so strengthen yourself that you can lift above the physical body, transcend all physical limitations, and in your knowingness, *be* in the higher levels of consciousness. You will know that you are there and you will know who else is there. You will know it as fully and completely as you know the lower levels. It will be your reality, your base, your foundation. From that position, you come back to this level and handle your daily experiences."

Prayer then becomes like the pole vault that lifts us over the bar of our constricted, physical reality to the other side. In prayer, we can go beyond our limited perspective and connect to our inner knowing. Prayer lifts the veil so that we can remember that we are spiritual beings in a human form, and therefore, we are never alone. This practice gives us the foundation to go about our lives in a state of attunement, alignment, and greater clarity. We start to experience ourselves in a steadier, calmer, and more elevated state of being. We feel grounded in our spirit and at home in our bodies on this earth. We feel safe to take risks, to ask for what we want and need, and to reach out. We stop living life in fear, judgment, separation, and worry. We let go and become fully present in our lives.

I have seen the miracles of prayer in my life and in the lives of others. I have seen the power of prayer in action for those who believe that the call will be answered. Life can become full of grace, but we must be willing to go deep, through the sacred process of prayer. It never ceases to amaze me: when I am willing to surrender my ego to my higher power, I experience inner transformation. In this book, I am putting a spotlight on this heartfelt, God-given gift so that each one of us can embrace it in our own way and feel its power in our own lives.

You can pray in your bedroom, in your bathtub, at the gym, on the train, or anywhere you choose. Prayer has nothing to do with location, religion, or ethnicity and everything to do with the human spirit that lives in all of us. If you are someone who doesn't spend time in a church, a temple, or a mosque, I invite you to read this book to explore the master key that we have all been given, to open the door to our connection with the ever-present spirit. We all long for this connection, like we may long to reunite with a long-lost lover, but because we are never taught how to find it in ourselves, we go out into the world looking for it and are left feeling empty and lonely.

The world will never remind us who we truly are. The way we live and function is a trap to forget our true nature. Our culture constantly signals to us that we're valued according to our accomplishments, finances, education, and even appearance. Most of us live in deficit. We constantly *do* so that we don't *feel* that sense of deficiency. We are superconnected to the external world, but we neglect to cultivate and connect to our internal world. When we turn inward, we experience an emptiness because we haven't spent enough time there to open up the inner domain of the spirit. So we withdraw from our souls. We start to feel displaced, wondering why we are here on earth after all and longing for deeper connection.

That's where prayer comes in. When we pray, we are not praying to someone or something outside of ourselves. We pray to the deeper, wiser, higher, and more intelligent part of ourselves that is connected to the whole. We pray to the awakened part of ourselves that is indeed the God in us. All we are asked to do is gently turn toward it and listen. Prayer, then, is the quiet focus that connects us to the inner knowing that we are not deficient in anything. You will go about your daily life from a place of fullness, aligned with your higher purpose, spirit-led. Think of prayer as your inner compass, pointing you in the direction you need to travel with a sense of confidence and strength. This deeper connection is available to each and every one of us, 24-7, just like our breath.

My prayer for you is that this book will serve as your guide to your inner resource. I pray that you discover the invaluable gift of prayer for yourself, and dissolve any illusion of separation between yourself and the presence within you.

Eight Billion Ways to Pray

There are hundreds of ways to kneel and kiss the ground.
—RUMI

Here are some things to consider as you bring the intimate practice of prayer into your everyday life. First, allow yourself to come into receptivity and open your heart to receive the inner guidance. Quiet the mind and start to fall inward so you can listen. Set your ego aside and become more vulnerable so you can experience the shift, hear the guidance, and start to receive the awareness. Be grateful for having the willingness and the openness to allow the higher self to emerge and present itself to you. As you open yourself, you will start to experience a deep quiet in order to listen. Your mind will settle, your emotions will start to reset, and your heart will expand. It's a feeling of reverence.

In prayer, you begin moving beyond the confines of the self that is preoccupied with so many things. Whoever you think you are, you are not. Because our thinking is finite, we cannot conceive with our minds the soul of who we are, which is infinite. The power in the process of prayer is that you go beyond your thoughts and your restricted mind, and you start to touch upon the reality of who you really are. It is as if the curtain is slowly being lifted, and there you are! From that place, you can ask, listen, and commune. It's like the story of the monk who kept asking God, "What can I do to serve you?" One day, his inner voice said, "Shut up and let me love you." When you are in the presence, you might realize that you need nothing. The loving presence in you knows your yearnings, your longings, and your wants, and they are being answered.

As Rumi wrote, "You are not a drop in the ocean, you are the entire ocean in a drop." As you pray, you are returned to that ocean within you. Your mere willingness to go into that state of reverence allows this to unfold. You will then emerge in your fullness.

There are eight billion people on earth and eight billion ways to pray. Prayer does not limit itself to form. Homer, the great poet, sang for his heroes in the epics *The Iliad* and *The Odyssey*. Aren't these forms of prayer? Rumi, Hafiz, and Kabir wrote endless poems and odes to the inner lover. John Lennon wrote the song "Imagine," and wasn't that a beautiful prayer for humanity? Beethoven wrote "Ode to Joy." Michelangelo created the beautiful and awe-inspiring statue of David. Those were their prayers. What will yours be? Whatever moves your soul, inspires your awe, and awakens your spirit can be prayer. It doesn't matter how you pray, only that you do. Let your heart take the lead and be your loving guide.

You can pray in any state of being. Start exactly where you are.

You don't have to stand in ceremony or be in your Sunday best. It's not complicated, and it doesn't have to be ritualistic. It can be simple: "Please help me find my way. Please restore me to my health. Please heal my heart to know love again. Please lift my spirit." Pray when you are tired and need energy. Pray when you are drinking a cup of coffee and thinking about the day ahead. Pray when you are waiting for the bus. Pray when you are on hold with a travel agent. Pray when you are on a deadline and don't think you're going to make it. Pray when you are stuck and feeling uninspired. Pray that your children will grow to become who they are meant to be. Pray for their classmates and their teachers. Pray for the discipline to stay focused on your purpose. Pray for the willingness to release resentment or anger. Pray when you are satisfied and when you are dissatisfied, when you are grateful and when you are wanting. Pray when you are picking up your kids from school, when you have an argument with your significant other, when your mortgage is overdue, when a friend lies to you and you feel betrayed. Pray that your heart and your gifts will be of service to those around you. Don't save prayer for special occasions. Whatever each moment presents is your portal for opening yourself to prayer. Pray for everything and every situation!

Is it possible that prayer can create such a powerful shift in your life? It is. For some, two minutes of prayer can make a difference. For others, it might take daily practice. I believe that it depends on how open you are to receiving the inner guidance and inspiration that will come to you. It requires a willingness to give up control. Even at our most miserable, the last thing human beings want is to give up control. If, at these moments when we are at our most resistant, we make the choice to surrender to prayer, we will find the support we are looking for. You can live your whole life with clenched fists, willing yourself forward, suffering the illusion that you are in control. Or you can live your life with open hands and an open heart, allowing the spirit to co-create with you and lead you in everything you do, walking with a feeling of peace, at home with yourself. This is the gift of prayer. The choice is yours.

How to Use This Book

In this book, I have compiled prayers according to themes we all deal with in our lives. My wish for you is that this book will serve as your guide to harnessing the power of prayer in your own life, offering you the words until you find your own.

When you read the prayers in this book, try reading them out loud. There is healing energy in our own voices, and hearing your own voice activates the spirit in us in a way that is moving and transformative. Add your own words, your own intention. Gradually, you'll start to experience the stillness, peace, and serenity that can come with knowing how to connect with your own presence. The spirit of God is in you, not outside of you. As you reflect upon that, you are filled with awe. You don't have to go anywhere to connect with that presence. Just be here right now, wherever you are, in whatever state you find yourself—vulnerable, unadorned, in your humanness and all that goes with it. Show up as you are in the moment without pretense and lay yourself bare; trust that there is a place within yourself that offers unconditional love. If I ever got a tattoo, I would engrave on my forehead: "God is your partner," to remind all of us that we are never alone. Prayer is a direct channel to God at all times and is as close as our next breath. It is our invisible support system.

Think of prayer as your favorite kite with the string wrapped around the spool that you're holding in your hands. You are the one that releases the string for the kite to fly. When you're flying a kite, the wind can take you in many directions. In the same way, your emotions, your thoughts, and whatever you're going through in your life can sway you from one direction to another until you steady yourself—until the kite, the wind, and you become one. Then, you can fly as high as you want.

I

Living

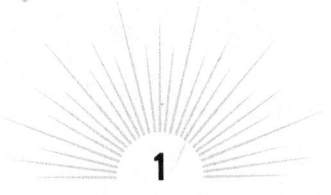

1

My Birthday Wish: May My Life Be an Offering

My birthday is on March 21, the first day of spring, and has always been a very special day for me. When I was a little girl, my mother always celebrated my birthday in the most wonderful ways. I would wake up in the morning to balloons, ribbons, and, of course, tons of food. There was always a party in the afternoon with all my friends: I was the center of attention, and I felt seen and loved—I mattered. Even when I was living on my own in London, the tradition continued; I celebrated my birthday, no matter what. I always gathered with friends, went out to dinner, and felt an abundant joy in the celebration of my life.

Later, when I lived with my sister at our home in Los Angeles, we would invite my spiritual teacher, John-Roger, and a few other friends, and we would sit around a table expressing our wishes, blessings, and prayers. It was magical!

One year, I came up with the wish to live life for a day in the true freedom of my spirit: a day with no judgments or self-imposed limitations; a day with a sense of peace and joy; a day to experience the freedom of my soul and my connection to the light. So, that became my new birthday tradition. To me, that would be the best birthday present ever, and there were some birthdays when my wish came true—I felt a fullness in my heart and an exuberant joy, I was free of any worries or preoccupations tugging at me, and I was totally present in my happiness—so I had a powerful reference point for the rest of my days.

In 2020, my birthday found me in Los Angeles. It was the second week of the coronavirus pandemic, and I was in quarantine.

Obviously, this was going to be a very different kind of a birthday celebration, one spent at home cooking with my family, who I was quarantined with, and connecting with friends via FaceTime and text—different ways of receiving love from my friends and family. Although I was saddened that I could not have people come for dinner, get my hair done, or go to my favorite restaurant, I woke up that morning filled with such profound gratitude that my family and I were at home together, safe and healthy. In the midst of the crisis, I felt a sense of fullness without any external celebration. In the context of the pandemic, it was most important to be with those I love the most—my family. The day was not only about celebrating me and my birthday, but also about our togetherness and our immense gratitude that we were healthy and well.

I experienced a deep sense of compassion for people across the world because of what they were suddenly enduring: businesses and cities were shutting down, people were losing family members, many were losing their jobs, and everyone was facing immense uncertainty about the future. I wanted to fall to my knees and thank God for my life and for a moment of goodness in the face of all that was happening. The week before, I had been preoccupied with which restaurant we should go to for my birthday dinner and whether I would have time to buy a new outfit to wear. Just one week later, life shifted into perspective. I was overcome with the feeling that there was nothing to get but everything to give back.

This heartfelt connection to the soulfulness of life has always been with me, but it was activated in a new way on this recent birthday. That morning, there was this resonant deep prayer inside of me: "I want more of you, God, and less of me." All of us, on some level, suffer from feelings of deficiency and lack, and we are always seeking validation outside of ourselves. But we are holding the key to the door through which we can find validation. That validation is directly connected to realizing we are created from the essence of the spirit. When we tune in to that reality, of course we will automatically feel validated because we understand the wholeness of who we are spiritually. You might be a mess in your physical reality, but there is always a loving soul inside of you. The soul doesn't wait until you think you have it all together to love you. The soul wants to love you right now, just as you are. If you pray for access to that source, it will overflow into the rest of your life.

That birthday morning, I got to the place of knowing that life had given me so much. I was hit with this recognition of the richness of my life, and I prayed to make my life an offering to that larger spirit, to hold that intention on a daily basis, and to become more attuned to how I can be of service and add to the good of all.

Ask yourself: What would your life be like if you really gave up the things that hold you back from experiencing your fullness and the aliveness of your spirit? What is the one thing you could release so your soul could expand? Is it that you don't feel that you are enough; you don't feel loved or valued; you believe that other people's lives matter more than yours? Is it that you wish you were more successful, more attractive, more recognized, more financially secure, more confident, more supported by others, more seen? Can you find a place within yourself in which you can let go of these feelings and instead embrace the gift that you are alive? In that moment of experiencing the miracle of your aliveness, you will see yourself as the beloved, and you will let your soul fill you with the light and love of who you are. You will be less worldly driven and more spirit-filled.

It doesn't have to be your birthday. You can make this wish at any time—to become more aware of the beauty, light, and inner mastery that is the birthright of each one of us waiting to be revealed. I believe that the power of our transformation is not in the big things but in the small ways we can let go and open ourselves to the greater presence within us.

It takes courage to take the first step toward this unknown presence, not knowing when we ask if anything will be there to meet us or if we will be left hanging alone. I assure you that if you dive into your heart, and from that deep place, ask to be led, you will be guided by the spirit that lives inside of you.

The Prayer

Dear Beloved,

When my heart shifts my eyes to your gaze, my whole self releases and feels the calm parts of your spirit flow in me.

On my birthday, I make my life an offering to you. I give my life back to you!

I now let go of my ambition, my desire to become something more important than I am, my insecurity and my angst. I release them to your grace.

I am like the most divine circus ringmaster, taming my lesser parts that want more of this and more of that, and I open my arms and say to you, "I want more of you!" I now breathe you in, I am letting you in, and I kneel in the altar of love and immerse myself in the spirit of oneness.

I feel like an excited child, led by the most loving parent to the theme park, who is about to explore the rides, and even have fun on the roller coasters. My life belongs to you because, in fact, it was never mine. It was freely given to me. Now it is yours again, even more blossomed and fuller than before.

Thank you for this newfound liberation that comes with knowing that love can flow in me and from me again, so I may touch the hearts of others and be of joyful service.

So be it.

2

How to Dial the
Spirit for Directions

Every day, we are all faced with choices that we have to make about our lives: health, finances, relationships, homes, work, kids, even what we're having for dinner. Often, we are conflicted, and not knowing which is the right choice leaves us in limbo. This is such a great opportunity to remind yourself that you can reach for your lifeline and dial the spirit for support and clarity. There is nothing too small to bring to the light.

When I was living with my family in Santa Barbara, my sister and her family decided to move to Washington, DC. I knew it was time for me to leave Santa Barbara as well, but I wasn't clear about my direction or what was next for me. I was dating a man who lived in New York, I had very little income, and I had interest from a publisher to write a book on the Greek goddesses. I kept being nagged to move to New York. I had lived there before, so I had friends there, and it was also where my spiritual community met to participate in different classes. There was plenty for me to do there, and I would be close to my family in Washington, but I still felt terrified. It was such a big change, so it felt like a big decision.

One night, before I went to sleep, I prayed and asked for guidance. I had a dream so vivid that I can still remember every detail. I was in a beautiful bedroom, and the man I was dating showed up and said to me, "My name is Baruch"—which isn't his name but is a Hebrew word that means "blessings"—"and I've come to invite you to New York with me. You can come by boat or you can come by plane, and you'll be taken care of in the way you have been accustomed to!" I woke up in the morning and it was clear as a bell: I was moving to New York! The spirit was directing me. I felt energized and excited in making the decision. I packed my things in Santa Barbara, and I moved to New York with a joyful heart, trusting that the way would be revealed to me.

Two months after I moved, I broke up with the man I was dating. I realized that he had served the purpose of bringing me to New York, where I discovered my confidence and strength and unleashed a newfound creative expression. I ended up living in New York for six years and became comfortable living on my own. I trusted that I was not alone; instead, I was guided, inspired, and supported by the light and the spirit. There were many difficult moments, many lonely times, and many times that I had to search for my courage, strength, and resilience. When I was writing my first book, I kept asking for help to break through my self-doubt and my fear; I kept opening up to new ways to tend to myself; I kept reaching in and reaching out to others for support. I found so many new ways to spread my wings, and I realized that there was a field of opportunities available as I kept discovering my connection to God in a daily and practical way. And my God, six years later, when I left New York to return to California, I was a different woman. I had written a book, built a whole body of work on the Greek goddesses archetypes, and explored so many new territories of myself that, under the canopy of my family, I could not have discovered.

So often, when we are asked to embark on new ventures, we are terrified by the unknown. But a new calling can be a golden opportunity to step into the fullness of who we truly are. It's like one of my favorite sayings: "Ships are safe in the harbor, but that's not what ships are made for." Our tendency, as human beings, is to stay safe and resist change, but in my experience, life pushes us toward change. Prayer can guide us out of the harbor to start sailing, even if we can't predict the weather.

Similarly, when I moved out of New York, a lot had changed. Both of my parents had passed away, my sister was now divorced and living in Los Angeles with her daughters, and she had asked me to live with her in LA. I was, again, so conflicted. How could I let go of the life I had created in New York, with friends I loved and a rhythm I was now accustomed to? My own rhythm?

During one of my spiritual classes, we took a field trip to a church in New York that had a labyrinth, also known as a maze. There is a beautiful ancient tradition in which you imagine an intention or a question addressed to your spirit, and then you walk the labyrinth. It is a metaphor for the journey to the center of your deepest self and back out into the world with a broadened understanding of who you are. As I was walking the labyrinth, I asked for clarity about the move back to Los Angeles. An image of a trapeze appeared inside of me, and I was shown that if I could let go, there would be someone on the other side to catch me. I laughed at how graphic and specific the spirit was. In that moment, I knew I had the willingness and the knowhow to take the leap. I remember being hit with such joy as I was packing my bags, so happy that I would be reunited with my sister and my two nieces, whom I so love and had missed living near. The terrified girl who had left Los Angeles six years be-

fore, thinking that she had found her dream man, was returning as a woman who had reconnected with her purpose.

So many times in my life I have been shown my direction
and helped in very specific ways. I want to encourage you, in
this prayer, to allow the higher wisdom of guidance to come
through in every little detail of your life. There is always going to
be unknown territory, and there are always going to be some insecurities, some trepidations, and the human part of you says,
"What do I do now? How do I proceed with the best choice?" If
you are willing to give that part of yourself over to your higher
consciousness, it is remarkable how you will be shown how to
proceed in very specific ways, tailored to you. We must be willing to listen to ourselves, to stop the noise and go beyond the
fear, to move toward an expanded sense of trust. There is a wise
voice in us that will always counsel us if we will just make room
for it to speak.

The Prayer

Dear Beloved,

*I quiet myself, and I ask that I may move into clarity and
receptivity so I may hear the voice of my wisdom in choosing
the proper and right decision for the situation. (Please add*

to this prayer the specifics of your personal situation for which you would like support.)

I am presented with various options, and as I consider these options, please guide me to make the right decision that is the perfect choice for me and my family's well-being.

As I move forward, I ask to keep the highest good of all concerned in mind.

Allow me to see what is most beneficial for me and not be distracted by my wishful thinking or the red flags and the pitfalls in my way—to see clearly where there is a greater opportunity for more joy, more peace, and less stress!

As I move forward, I ask that I may not let my fear stop me but that I may be guided by the hand of the higher, protective power that is for me! Let that guidance now give me a sense of strength and security, and a solid foundation to see the choice that will bring me greater productivity, greater alignment, and greater cooperation, always moving hand in hand with my higher self in this decision.

I want to trust myself and my intuition, move away from self-doubt and second-guessing, and let my divine presence be part of this choice. May I move into my fullness and choose what is right for me!

I claim my patience, remembering that there is no urgency in the spirit. I thank you for helping me move past my own limitations, my ego, and any parts of me that hold me back from knowing that I'm always guided. I always do know what is best for me and my life. I now give this decision over to the light within and I go free.

So be it.

It's Not a Trade; It's an Offering

And still, after all this time,
the sun has never said to the earth, "You owe me."
Look what happens with love like that. It lights up the sky.
— RUMI

During a gathering at a friend's house, a woman complimented my mother's pearl necklace. "I love your pearl necklace," she told her. At that point, my mother removed the necklace and handed it to the woman. "It's yours now," she told her. "Enjoy it." The woman was stunned. "But what can I give you in return?" she asked my mother. My mother responded, "It's not a trade, darling; it's an offering." This was how my mother lived, making every interaction a true offering.

So often, we live life as a trade. We do things for others, but then we expect them to do things for us. We see every interaction as a transaction, which robs us of authentic and heartfelt human connection. When we live this way, we start to take our lives for granted. But when we live life as an offering, the world around us takes on a different dimension as we start to live in gratitude for all that we receive.

So much is freely given to you. Think about everything that surrounds you and everything that you use every day and how every item you use represents the work of hundreds of people to produce and transport it. How humbling it is to consider. We are the recipients of so much. It is because of the many contributions that countless people make every day that this world becomes a place for us to partake of and enjoy.

Let us practice the muscle of gratitude so that we may live in the awareness of the chain of hands and minds and skills that it takes to produce everything around us. This mindfulness can be, in itself, a walking prayer.

The Prayer

Today, I turned on the faucet, and the presence of love touched my hand and said, "Think of the many miles this water had to travel from its source to reach you in your home. Think of the scientists who developed methods so that you don't have to walk miles for a bucket of water."

And I was grateful.

I turned on the switch, and the lights went on in my home, and the presence of love touched my hand and whispered, "Think of the miracle of electricity and the thousands of years in which humanity lived in the dark. Think of how, even today, millions of people in the world have no electricity, and every day, as the sun goes down, they have to find other ways to light their homes."

And I was grateful.

I hugged my friend as she hugged me, and I heard a whisper in my ear, "Think of all the people who haven't been hugged in years and years and are devoid of love, kinship, and companionship and have forgotten the warmth of human connection."

And I was grateful.

I sat down to eat and enjoy my meal, and as I was about to pick up my fork I felt the presence of love take me to the farms where seeds are planted and harvested so that fruits and vegetables can grow and be distributed to the markets and we can all enjoy them. I thought of the hundreds of people who worked so hard for me to have food on my table.

And I was grateful.

Then my mind wandered to so many things I do every day, which millions of people do, that are so easy for us to access. I heard the voice of my heart whisper, "Take a moment, every time you do something that is easy and accessible to you, and hold in reverence the gifts of your life. When you get the inner calling, aim to make your life an offering to all those around you and give thanks to all those you may never meet who contribute to your life every day."

Pray that you are used to your capacity and pray that you may never take the gift of life's abundance for granted, so you may always look at the world with a heart full of wonder and eyes full of awe. Every day, look up to the sun that creates the day and let your heart leap to touch the sunbeams with the deepest bow of thank you.

Quick God Fix for the Pressure of a Deadline or a Delay

Please help me expand the limitations of man's time and reach into the expansion of God's time.

4

The Sweetness of Doing Nothing

Greeks love to lounge. They are so good at it. They nap; they spend endless time chatting with one another; they linger over long meals. Unlike English and American cultures, the Greek culture has nothing fast about it. As a young girl, I remember seeing people resting by olive trees in the Greek countryside, eating their lunch at a leisurely pace, and I remember the beautiful holidays we would spend in the Greek islands by the sea, sunbathing, gazing, and taking in the beauty of our surroundings.

When I left my country to move to London, things changed. A new country, a new culture, and a new school created an insecurity in me about the purpose and direction of my life, which made it hard for me to enjoy times of rest. I woke up and went to sleep with this feeling of angst and restlessness. It takes tremendous discipline and wisdom to know how to settle in with yourself.

Fast forward a couple of decades after a lot of inner work—seminars, classes, retreats, and life itself (the greatest school of all)—and I'm happy to share with you that I'm now much better able to take time off to rest, to wonder, and to let myself be.

I was once on the island of Ithaca filming a documentary on the Greek gods, and I recall lying in my hotel room that overlooked the Mediterranean Sea, listening to the waves crash against the rocks as a breeze wafted through the room. It was midafternoon around four o'clock, and I felt this incredible feeling of ease come over me, as if my whole body, mind, and spirit sank into the bed. It was a profound moment of relaxation and connection at the same time, and it has stayed with me ever since. How wonderful it is to let the presence of rest take over. A call to rest often comes knocking at the door, and we have the choice of whether to let it in. Our mind will fight us by trying to tell us that we have too much to do or we will miss out on something, but what we miss out on by failing to rest is the wonderful feeling of replenishment and the decompression of our busy minds. In rest, we can go deeper to a place where we can relax and reemerge renewed.

I think the fundamental reason why we don't give ourselves permission to rest is that we are afraid to let go. As Steve Jobs so accurately described it, "If you just sit and observe, you will see how restless your mind is. If you try to calm it, it only makes it worse, but over time it does calm, and when it does, there's room to hear more subtle things—that's when your intuition starts to blossom and you start to see things more clearly and be in the present more. Your mind just slows down, and you see a tremendous expanse in the moment. You see so much more than you could see before." We are so driven to constantly move from one thing to the next so that we won't feel the anxiety, the worry, or the underlying uncertainty that we live with every day.

Even during the coronavirus pandemic, as I engaged and interacted with people via various forms of technology, I thought, "God, this could be an amazing opportunity to rest! No one can go anywhere." But no one was resting because their fears, insecurities, and vulnerabilities were amplified, and when we were closed up in our homes with limited access to the outside world, we were consumed by this restlessness even more.

Wherever you are right now, whatever state you're in, ask yourself these questions: Do I allow myself to rest, and what is my ideal way of resting? What is the first image that comes to mind when I think of rest, other than my bed? You can be in the countryside on a hammock, lying by a lake in a beautiful garden shifting between snoozing and reading a relaxing book, or walking on the beach as the sun sets. I believe rest occurs when we let ourselves be, when we truly enjoy our lives without the pressure of doing, achieving, accomplishing. It's like free-falling: you don't know where the next thought is coming from. Allow yourself to be taken by the sweetness of the spirit and enjoy the quiet of nature—the whistling of the trees, the expansiveness of the ocean, the feeling of your body lying in the grass.

We have a garden at our home in Los Angeles that has beautiful green grass, and I don't remember ever allowing myself to lie down in the grass and look at the sky. It wasn't until I wrote this chapter that I realized it was something I really wanted to do. I let myself be. I drifted and sank into the earth, my eyes gazing at the sky, and I let myself wonder, "How did it all happen, how did I happen, and what is beyond the earth that I cannot see? Isn't it amazing that, as I'm lying here on this grass, the earth is revolving around the sun so slowly that I can't even feel it?" I let myself breathe in the mystery of life.

The expansion and awe of that moment birthed this prayer for more magical moments of my own rest. I encourage you to write your own prayer with your own words about what rest means to you and step into the prayer of rest. Give yourself permission to go to that deeper place where your God-self will enter and reveal to you a greater state of grace in which to live.

The Prayer

Dear Beloved,

I now ask to be gifted rest.

I ask to know the power of pausing in my life.

I ask to be able to give myself permission and know that I have a right to rest, a right to wonder, a right to daydream, a right to let myself be—to do nothing but let my consciousness drift so I may see and receive the blessings that are there for me.

I dream and I ask for the feeling of a lazy summer afternoon, lying in the grass, looking at the sky, seeing the clouds go by, listening to the birds, and wondering at the majesty of the trees who have been there before me and will be there long after I am gone.

And I ask myself: When was the last time I ever did that and felt the presence in the summer breeze, yielded to your touch? Why am I so consumed by constant doings and fixings, by the management of my daily affairs? So much of that robs me of my joy and rest.

I feel like I may miss this or that—or even more, that I will be forgotten and left behind if I do not catch up and participate in the human "race." Help me believe that with the calm that comes with rest, I will arrive exactly where I need to be at the perfect time.

So now I bring myself to you, and I ask, with all my heart, show me how to do nothing, how to be calm in the face of the hustle and bustle of our world, and gift myself the grace of rest, knowing that the truth of who I am and the sweetness of my soul lies in that space of rest.

So be it.

The Gifts That Lie in the In-Between Times

During the coronavirus pandemic, we all had to pause—not out of choice but because of the demands of the crisis. Although it felt like life interrupted, it got me thinking about so many times in our lives when we are in-between experiences and phases.

Everything in life is cyclical, like the seasons. As a day ends and the evening begins, there is this transition when we are bridging the day into the night. When we are transitioning into a new phase of life, it can feel like the ground has disappeared from beneath us and we are falling into unstructured territory. You can grieve as you let go of the old, but preparing the ground for the new to come is a sacred process. It's important not to skip past the transition, as uncomfortable as it may be.

In my own life, an in-between time came at a very specific moment. I had spent about ten years developing a body of work on the archetypes of Greek gods and goddesses. I wrote a one-woman show that I performed at different venues, wrote two books, conducted numerous workshops, produced a PBS special, and created a jewelry line. I felt fulfilled in creating and producing those projects. Then I moved in with my sister and my two teenage nieces in Los Angeles, my parents were deceased, and I found that my work on the goddesses was complete. There wasn't any more juice. I didn't know what was coming next.

I did a lot of reflection and felt the trepidation of facing the blank canvas. Looking back, I realize that I was actually in a constant state of prayer, asking the spirit to give me new inspiration. One day, I was introduced to a young actor who wanted help with her career; very much like me when I was her age, she wasn't getting the roles she wanted. I had dinner with her and started to tell her my story: how I hadn't been getting the roles I wanted and felt that the doors of my acting career were closed. I had to find my own creative spark and ended up developing the one-woman show on the goddesses. As I was telling her my story, I saw how incredibly impacted she was. She told me that my story needed to be shared.

At that moment, as I saw how my experience could help

someone else, I realized the impact of patiently and kindly listening to our inner direction to see where life is taking us. I was being led to write *Unbinding the Heart,* my book in which I share my story and reflect on my life experiences. In that process, I came to see how the in-between times and the times of reflection can be just as important as the "doing" times. That book led me to doing my life's work, which is authentically sharing my own experiences from my heart and inspiring other people to connect to their soul's purpose, to use everything in their lives to become who they're meant to be.

In-between times can come in many forms. If you let go of a relationship, you then have time and space to reflect on your own about what worked, what didn't work, what you would like more of. But if you rush into another relationship, you might find that you are repeating the same pattern. If you let go of a job and are looking for something new and more exciting and engaging, you have to take time and find the courage to embark on new creativity, reach out and brainstorm with people, and be mentored by people you respect.

One of the greatest lessons we all must learn is letting go of control and the way we know ourselves so we can move into a new expansion of who we truly are. Often on that journey, we find that we resist the change, resist the unknown, resist feeling out of control, and it's very tempting to become pessimistic, negative, and discouraged. Yet, at those times, we can lean back and allow the greater spirit in us to be present—to open new inner doors, and maybe even outer doors, to new opportunities.

The Prayer

Dear Beloved,

I am in this period of in-between.

I ask that I may transform this period by allowing my patience, my self-compassion, and my trust in infinite possibilities into my life. I ask to release my impatience and my restlessness as I wait patiently to see what is next for me.

Whatever blessings are in store for me, I ask to see them and be in gratitude for what is in my life.

Let me tend to myself in practical ways by lovingly holding a safe space for myself and communicating to myself—my worries, my fears, my dislikes of how things are, my wants—and embracing all that, so I can take all of me in and begin to feel trust in the face of not knowing. Replace my negative thinking with the joy of all that is to come.

Instead of focusing on the lack and absence of what is not here, I ask that I may return to my soulfulness and allow my vulnerability to come forward. As I open and expand instead of contract, I will discover more deeply the presence of my soul, hear my wisdom, and let my tenderness fill me up.

As I'm letting go of control, I want to experience the inner freedom of letting go and letting God in.

So be it.

Prayer for Time Running Out

Dear Beloved,

I have been feeling the pressure of time, the feeling that I am running out of time. As I move from one thing to another throughout my day, lying under this nagging feeling of wanting to do things faster and better—and needing to complete all these things in a single day—is the fear that time is running out.

Assist me and guide me so I may know that, in this moment, with my own breath and with the consciousness of being present in my breath, there is timelessness and expansion.

Although the reality is that time has a speed to it and moves to its own rhythm, I ask that I may stay connected to my own time, my own breath, and that, in this moment, as

I move from one thing to another, I can still be at peace with time.

I don't need to have urgency or succumb to the imprisonment of time. Instead, I ask that I may expand with the spirit within that lives beyond the limitations of time.

I ask that I may see the perfection in how everything is unfolding, and know that the greater reality of spirit exists beyond the illusion of time.

Now, as I exhale, I start to find my inner flow and break the restrictions of how I relate to time, and instead I experience my inner freedom.

I embrace this time, I make the best of it, and most of all, I bring the fullness of my compassion, my joy, and my love to it. Thank you.

So be it!

6

God, Help Me Laugh Again!

Do you remember when you were younger and would laugh at the silliest things? That's the kind of joy that I want in my life. I often ask the spirit for that joy in the middle of a situation that feels heavy or stuck. To give me a lightness of being when I'm exercising, cooking, or writing, I ask that I can find that mirth, which is really a connection with the spirit.

Hafiz wrote a book titled *I Heard God Laughing,* and in it he wrote, "Start seeing everything as God, but keep it a secret." I think that's what brings lightness to our being: seeing situations that we, as humans, take so seriously, including ourselves, through God's eyes. What does that mean? It means that you are freer and more expansive, less preoccupied with yourself, your circumstances, and your inner angst. It means that you're less wrapped up in the drama of life and more in tune with the humor of life.

Scientists estimate that the average person has about sixty thousand thoughts per day, and of those thoughts, 80 percent are negative and 95 percent are repetitive. No wonder we struggle to find our joy. We wrap our souls in restrictive patterns and habits, but what loosens and finally dissipates those confines is a higher perspective. It's in our nature to base our happiness on what happens, what doesn't happen, and the results of those events or the attention we get from others. But with prayer, we can find the river of light and the joy of being alive inside. As Hafiz wrote, "I am happy even before I have a reason."

Soon after I moved to New York and rented a beautiful one-bedroom apartment, it was my birthday. Since I was a little girl, I was used to my mother orchestrating a special celebration for my birthday, but she was in Los Angeles at the time, so I decided to throw myself a party with all my friends. I now refer to that party as my French-farce birthday. Everything that could have gone wrong, went wrong. I made an appointment for a haircut, and my hairdresser became sick and canceled at the last minute. I went to a shop to meet a friend who wanted to buy me a dress as a birthday present. When we arrived at the shop, there was a sign saying it had permanently closed! I ordered Greek food to serve my guests, but when the food arrived, it was in tin-foil containers, and I didn't have serving platters. So I decided to ring the bells of my neighbors' apartments, introduce myself for the first time as the new tenant, and ask them if they had any platters that I could borrow. I can't imagine what they thought when they opened the door and saw me standing there, desperate for serving platters! A new ottoman was delivered, days after it was meant to arrive, and I had no clue how to assemble it, so I had to frantically call the building superintendent and ask if he could help me.

By the time the party was to begin, let's just say I was not in the right state of mind to receive my guests. I was extremely stressed, but as soon as my friends started to arrive, I realized these were real friends, and I didn't have to impress anybody. I had a boyfriend at the time who arrived with a beautiful cold bottle of champagne. We opened it and got into the spirit of the occasion. My joy started to come back. I played music, ate food off of plates lent to me by my new neighbors, and ended up sharing the events of the day and telling my guests how every-thing went awry. At that point, one of my friends spilled a glass of red wine on my new white couch, and I felt that my French-farce birthday was complete. It's so liberating and refreshing when we can break loose from the seriousness of our lives and find levity in the moment, even when life is going in the opposite direction from how we want it to go.

Praying and asking, in every moment of our lives, to wake up to the joy of the soul is a remarkable way to bring more of that energy into each day. It can be a silent prayer for which you stand under a tree and say, "God I want to laugh a lot today. Show me things that can happen that bring out my laughter," and make that a silent intention to invite more of your joyful spirit into your life. Laughter boosts immunity, lowers stress hormones, decreases pain, relaxes your muscles, prevents heart disease, eases anxiety, and so much more. So, let us pray for laughter!

The Prayer

Dear Beloved,

I want to hear your laughter inside of me. I want to hear your mirth breaking through my seriousness and human restrictions, and find childlike joy, as if I'm twirling around for no reason, giggling and laughing inside, no matter what.

I ask to release my burdens—the thoughts, the judgments, the pressures that I feel—and, in their place, hear the bells, the tambourine, and all the instruments that bring joy to life.

No matter what's happening outside in my world, let me be fully present in my life and bubble over with joy so that others can feel it too. Show me the antidote to my negative and ruminative thoughts that can bring me down, so, as they arise, I can create distance between them and myself, reminding me that I am not those thoughts, and I am not my emotions, but I am the essence of life and the spirit of life is joyful.

I ask to find that part of me, despite the fact that life tells me it is serious and I should be serious. We all have this joy and laughter inside, so please show me how to access it and give myself permission to experience it.

Let me find entertainment, situations, shows, and friends who awaken the joy and the laughter in me, so I may become a conduit for joy.

Let us, you and me, laugh together and create more laughter, more mirth, more joy, more fun, more celebration for no reason other than the fact that we are alive.

So be it.

7

Finding the Extraordinary in the Ordinary

My favorite film quote is from *Chariots of Fire*. The protagonist, Eric Liddell, is training to run in the 1924 Olympic Games while preparing for a trip to China to work as a missionary. His sister admonishes him for not following God's will and says to him, "You have to throw away this silly running thing, and do this really important work, God's work." Eric looks at her and says, "But when I run, I feel his pleasure."

The other day I was listening to a wonderful podcast by Tim Ferriss, who was interviewing Hugh Jackman. Tim asked Hugh when he first knew that he was meant for the stage. Jackman answered with that same quote from *Chariots of Fire*. He said it was his favorite line because it describes how he feels when he is performing, the feeling of serving something larger than himself. I was so elated to be reminded of this quote about feeling God's pleasure. To me, God's pleasure occurs when the human part in us meets the miraculous spirit in us, and we have a moment in which our human self merges with our divine self.

I think we've all felt that connection in some way or another. It might be when we're dancing, singing, writing, cooking, walking up a mountain, watching a beautiful sunset, playing a sport, or even gardening. My mother would experience it on the beach while feeding the seagulls. They would all come flooding into her presence while she fed them bread crumbs. It was magical to witness.

I feel it when performing. Although I moved from acting to speaking and writing, I accessed that tremendous fulfillment as I went around the country speaking, inspiring, and sharing the message of the open heart and the joy that is innate in all of us. I never fail to experience the magic of our oneness when I speak. At each event, strangers and I bond, heart to heart. I go beyond the words on the page into the experience of being in the moment, speaking spontaneously from my heart and wisdom. Often, at the end of an event, people approach me and say, "What you said was meant for me. I felt my heart burst open. I really let go of something." I always feel the magical connection of my human self with the larger spirit. I leave every event feeling fulfilled and blissful, in awe of the expansion of the human heart. It is beyond anything I can describe. When I speak, I feel his pleasure!

Cut to the pandemic quarantine, when there were no events but endless Zoom calls. For me, it felt like I had been pushed out of my paradise, deprived of the very things I love the most. I meditated, I prayed, and I tried to find ways to recreate some of the feelings that I've had when speaking and connecting in real life. Those feelings never left me; I just needed to find ways to keep igniting that connection. I often thought of the thousands of actors, dancers, musicians, and singers who feel that aliveness when they perform, and I was filled with compassion and heartache when realizing they may have felt cut off from their joy during the pandemic. I tried to find it through dancing, moving, loving, listening to music, walking on the beach, connecting with my friends, and engaging in my work. But most of all, I found it through gratitude and reverence for the ordinary things of life.

When you can't access your favorite way to feel his pleasure, you're called to go deeper. Without judging, in the most loving and tender way, I say to myself, "I understand. I hear you. I'm here for you." I can find the connection in the stillness, in the gaze that sees into the soul of who I am and who others are. Maybe now I can find his pleasure in the deep quiet, beyond my restless and impatient mind that asks, "When will this end?" I can find his pleasure in the simplest, most ordinary things—feeling the breeze, smelling the roses, cooking a meal, feeling the sun's warmth on my skin, hearing the voices of my family in the other room—and magnify the gratitude of every ordinary moment with the spirit that lives in me and all of us, regardless of the conditions. It takes more stillness to hear the subtle whisper of the voice of the spirit that says, "I am still here. I never left. I'm never going anywhere, and you can feel me and find me as you stop looking back to what was, and instead open up your heart to experience what is now."

Suddenly, everything settles and the waves meet the shore. Whether it is a cloudy, sunny, rainy, or windy day, the waves will always meet the shore because that is the extraordinary, miraculous nature of all things. When we go beyond that which we feel we are missing or lacking, and focus instead on all that we have, the only response is simple awe. When we are in awe, then we can feel his pleasure with every breath and in every moment, as we bear witness to our aliveness that connects us to all life everywhere. When you live your life from that place, you are inside the extraordinary nature of your soul, and you will find the extraordinary in the ordinary of every day.

The Prayer

Dear Beloved,

One of the greatest joys in my life is feeling your presence as I connect with others by speaking, inviting other people to participate in my heart's expansion. Recently, I've been feeling the absence of my connection with you and feel I am lacking in that magic from which I converge with my spirit.

I ask now that I may find new ways to engage, move my body, be present in the miracle of my life, and awaken to the aliveness that I have in me.

I ask that I may remove the resistance, limitation, and stubbornness of wanting things to be a certain way. When things don't happen that way, I cave in, shut down, and blame you, the world, and myself, and then fall into my doom. Instead, I ask that I may again find this magic in the ordinary—that everything in this world, as hard as it might seem, is still working.

For whatever reason, my ego and my sense of self move into righteous indignation, and God forbid I might miss the awe that I so seek in the simplest of things.

The trees still grow upward, and I'm able to walk on this earth through the law of gravity, and even that is a miracle.

The earth still moves around the sun in perfect motion, and how amazing is that? There are invisible worlds of millions of stars and planets that are all moving in perfect relation to one another, and they don't seem to collide. The ocean meets the shore in perfect rhythm, even when it's turbulent and stormy.

Let me wrap my mind around all of that, and know that I, too, have perfect harmony within me.

So be it.

Prayer for Finding Your Balance

Dear Beloved,

I am feeling frazzled and out of balance. Something has set me off and removed me from my center, and I would like to take a few moments to refocus on my true sense of being.

I ask that I come into acceptance of what just happened and be able to forgive—to look at the deeper issue that might surface for me, and then let it go.

I ask that any judgment that I have toward myself, the other person, or the situation be forgiven.

I ask that I may not take everything personally right now, and that I may restore my love and acceptance for myself and recognize that what just happened doesn't mean there is anything wrong with me.

In this healing process, I ask and I permit that I may be able to transform from the experience of being out of balance to bringing the spirit in to restore me, let it go, and come into my own fullness.

I breathe in this balance. I breathe in my centeredness and let go.

I allow my feelings to surface to restore myself into my own balance by not denying how I feel, but knowing that there is me beyond my feelings, and that's the part that I want to connect with more.

So be it.

8

The Courage to Give All Parts of Yourself a Voice

It's so important to keep your internal channels of communication open, especially during times of crisis. We often function in our familiar patterns, going on autopilot from one thing to the next, accomplishing things in our daily lives. But a lot of feelings surface during the day, especially in challenging times. You may feel overwhelmed, upset, disconnected, worried, fearful, or out of control. Addressing all your emotions, and finding ways to give them a voice, will let you experience greater calm.

As adults, we have learned to censor our feelings of discontent, although some of us might vent them to or project them onto other people. But these feelings can give us important information. For instance, when you pray, there might be a part of yourself that says, "I don't believe that prayer really works, and I don't trust that there is anyone listening to me." If you listen to that voice and allow it expression, you will learn about yourself. You, in your wisdom, can address that part of yourself like a mother to a child, bringing love and compassion and guidance to that part of yourself so it can learn how to trust again. Or there might be a part of you that is angry because you didn't stand up for yourself at work or in a relationship, and that part of you is withholding energy from your being. When you let that part speak to you and really listen to it, you might ask for forgiveness. You might say, "I understand and I'm learning how you want me to protect you and stand by you."

Suddenly, you realize that you have your inner family. Most of us live in homes within our minds and hearts in which the doors of certain rooms are closed. We need to open those doors and let the light in to allow open communication among all parts of ourselves. When we do that, we find that we are more expansive in our sense of ourselves. In order to build a trusting relationship with the God in you, you have to have a trusting relationship with yourself, with all parts of you:

the child, the adult, the scaredy-cat, the ego, the discouraged person, the reluctant person, the shy person, and all the others. If we can start the conversation among the many parts of ourselves without judging them, we will sit in a consciousness of alignment because we are not withholding any energy from ourselves.

As wonderful as it is to have a therapist, coach, counselor, or even a loving friend, sometimes the *most* loving voice is available to us from within, but it takes courage to open up to yourself. Build the practice of connecting with yourself every day. You might feel vulnerable when your guard falls down and you reach the raw parts of yourself that have no defenses. You may resist that because the ego likes to feel in control and thrives on pretending it knows everything. Well, that's too bad because when life brings us abrupt changes we are forced to let go, re-evaluate our ego positions, and find new ways to engage in our lives. Most of the time we have to give up our false sense that we are in control. When we access the stillness inside of us, with the spirit on our side, we have the strength and the willingness to listen to ourselves. In prayer, we can open our hearts to the well of love and compassion and give ourselves permission to be so very human.

I keep a journal by my bedside, and at night, I answer three questions.

1. What worked today?

Sometimes the answers are very simple things, sometimes they are bigger things. For example, I reached out to a friend when I was feeling disconnected, or I was able to be there for a friend who was in need. Sometimes they are the simple things of daily life: taking a walk first thing in the morning or powering down my devices a few hours before bed and making sure not to watch the news too late at night. Ask yourself: What worked for me today?

2. What would I like to bring more of into my life?

This is an opportunity to hear all the parts of yourself. Maybe you are yearning for more playfulness in your life. Maybe you need the courage to hear something that has been buried inside of you. Just as a loving mother doesn't say to a child, "Shut up, we don't have time for that," listen to yourself with love and give each need an expression and a safe place.

3. What does the spirit have to say to me?

On this question, I pause, I listen, and I become very quiet, and the answer comes, not from my head but from the deeper part within me—my wise voice—that gives all parts of me guidance and direction.

Answering these three questions makes me aware of what's working and not working and allows me to listen for the deeper voices within me.

As you pray, you open up to all parts of yourself, not just the parts you have learned to lead with. Spirit doesn't judge the parts of us that may be resentful or discouraged or afraid or in doubt. On the contrary, the spirit wants to support and guide us through these difficulties. That's the beauty of prayer: the spirit meets us in our most human parts.

The Prayer

Dear Beloved,

I ask for the light to protect me, fill me, and surround me. I ask that the parts of me that have felt shut down, ignored, or withdrawn be given a voice. I ask for the willingness to give myself permission to listen to them.

I open up to all parts of myself and ask for the courage to look at all of myself without judgment. If there are parts that feel defeated, unworthy, betrayed, or pushed aside, I ask that the light shine on those parts so that they can open up and speak with me and through me, and give me information about what they want more of. Is it the strength and confidence to ask for what I want? Is it expression and creativity? Is it a willingness to ask for and receive help from others in my difficult times? Is it to know that I can have more joy in my life? Is it to better listen to and take care of myself?

I ask to bridge the gap between my human self and my wise self, so that I feel more whole, more integrated, and more comfortable in my vulnerability.

I want to get to know me, not who I think I am or should be, but who I really am in the deepest parts of myself. I allow my heart to open to all parts of myself so that I may know that I deserve to be unconditionally loved. In that, I receive the freedom and the ease that comes from knowing that all of me is worthy of expression and of love. I give up feeling like the victim and rise to feel like a warrior.

So be it.

9

Putting the Day to Rest

I am a night owl. I love the night. I feel reluctant to put the day to rest for many reasons. I love life so much that when I go to sleep, I feel like I'm missing out on undistracted time with myself and whatever it is I want to read or write or look at. At the end of the day, I have leftover energy that leaves me feeling awake. It is a pattern that I have tried to overcome because I like to wake up in the morning feeling rested and renewed.

I'm not alone in this habit. There are night owls and there are larks—night owls tend to sleep from around 2:00 a.m. to 10:00 a.m., and larks tend to sleep from around 10:30 p.m. to 6:30 a.m. I have always envied the morning people who wake up filled with energy and enthusiasm, and then off they go to the gym. We night owls must be disciplined and negotiate how much of the night we can have and how much of it we must learn to sacrifice.

I've always felt that at night, when I fall asleep, my spirit leaves my body. I go to some other place that is much more expansive than this three-dimensional reality. I experience some resistance when entering the body again in the morning, and of course, if I kept myself up at night, it's even harder.

I live with my sister, who is a sleep evangelist; she is highly disciplined about getting eight hours of sleep. She has a cutoff time for reading her emails and using technology, and she has made a practice of disconnecting and letting herself unwind for at least thirty minutes before bed each night. Often, these are her last words to me: "Make sure you turn off your devices and go to sleep" and "You are the one that declares the day complete." I have a saying framed on my desk: "A good day starts the night before."

But I still love the night, when everything is quiet, when there are no demands—inner or outer. I feel that the night belongs to me. So, this is my prayer for anyone who finds themselves thinking: "Did I get enough done? Will I miss something if I go to sleep? Do I deserve to rest? Can I let go, trusting that tomorrow will be there for me to complete what didn't get done today?" I often say this prayer to fall asleep with gratitude and self-appreciation. Go to sleep listening to soothing music, writing in your journal, praying, stretching, and if you have a partner next to you, sharing a moment of love and appreciation. Try to find it in your heart to go to sleep smiling, and make a practice of going to bed in peace.

In a dream, in a vision of the night,
when deep sleep falls upon men, while slumbering on their beds,
then He opens the ears of men and seals their instruction.
—JOB 33: 15–16

The Prayer

Dear Beloved,

I allow myself to lie my body down, to take a deep, long, slow breath, and exhale the day away.

I did the best I could with all that was on my plate.

There were no catastrophes, no earthquakes, nothing that shook the earth except what happened in my mind, so now I let my mind rest and unravel and discard what didn't go my way, and I give myself permission to soften my heart and take in the good.

All is well; what's left undone will be done tomorrow.

I declare it a good day—a day that emerged with all its ups and downs.

For any parts of myself that feel the judgments, longings, frustrations, fears, worries about those I love, and all the indecisions of my life, I lay them down to rest. I offer them to the higher light in me.

Whatever is stuck, hurt, or unfulfilled, let it be dissolved in the grace of the night.

In my dreams, show me, guide me, and instruct me on everything I need solutions for, and help me open the channel to receptivity so that I may receive my wisdom, my soulfulness, and my power to create the life I want for me and those I love.

Show me in my dreams that I am not alone, that I am always guided.

Let me put the day to rest and sleep in perfect harmony. So be it.

II

Creating

10

Reviving Your Enthusiasm for Each New Day

Have you ever gone to bed feeling empty and drained, dreading the next day? You feel that you have nothing to look forward to because you know that tomorrow will only bring more of the same. You feel a little bit like Bugs Bunny when he's been run over by a truck. But remember, Bugs Bunny gets up, shakes himself off, and gets back to work!

A lot of our lives revolve around routine and repetition, and we can get stuck in a rut. We go to work, we do the chores, we run the errands—all without renewed enthusiasm. There are, of course, chapters of our lives that are more creative, exciting, and expansive, but most of life is repetitive and can begin to feel monotonous. If we don't exercise the muscle of renewal, it atrophies. We lose the magic, the gratitude, and the beauty of our lives.

When we feel this way, it's because we have turned off the faucet: the channels of communication to the spirit. Everything about our lives feels humdrum and dry, and we don't feel we are being nourished. If you are feeling this way, remember you are in charge of the faucet. In these moments, we need to turn the faucet back on, so we can experience greater connection and a sense of renewal, even as we do the same things day-to-day. All that is required of you is a willingness to be present in this moment in which you are alive.

Where does this sense of renewal come from? It comes from the awareness that the aliveness of the spirit is always with us. Take a few moments for reflection and silence. Stop running from one thing to the next. Nothing is more important than you receiving renewed energy. Give yourself a break from your routine, wherever you are. During any moment that feels monotonous or humdrum, you can pause and ask for renewal, ask for reconnection with the spirit within you, and ask for awareness of yourself as a spiritual being. What are the things you can do to make this day a brand new day? In any moment, we can renew ourselves by drawing upon the creative spiritual presence, which is always in the present.

I was once driving from Los Angeles to Santa Barbara, and I

was in a funk. As I drove down the highway, I felt pulled to drive to the ocean. I pulled off of the highway and parked in front of the ocean and just looked at it. As I sat there, my favorite piece of music, "The Blue Danube" by Johann Strauss, came on the radio. I started to cry. I was overtaken by a tremendous release of pent-up feelings, lingering disappointments, and a general feeling of despair. I just needed to cry. I felt the light come in and lift me and comfort me. I had clarity that everything would be okay. But the key here is that the spirit prompted me to do something—drive to the ocean—and instead of ignoring it, I listened. That listening opened me up to the assistance that was available to me. At times like that, what we really crave is the reassurance that we are not alone. The problem is not so much in the details of our lives, but rather in our emotional and spiritual experience of our lives. If we don't draw on the spiritual energy that is within us, life becomes drudgery.

In writing this book, you have no idea how many times I had to renew my enthusiasm for the project. The introduction that you read at the beginning of the book went through twelve drafts! When my energy flagged, I prayed. When we pray to the spirit, we can ask to receive renewed energy and creativity. Lin-Manuel Miranda, the brilliant playwright/composer of *Hamilton*, was asked how he maintains such outrageous creativity day-to-day. He answered, "I get up every day and remind myself

outrageous creativity

that tomorrow is not promised, so I only have today. And I give it my all." That is such a wonderful way to live: remembering that tomorrow is not promised. When we summon our energy to be present in the moment and overcome the fear to feel our feelings—to speak them, to cry about them, to express them in all our vulnerability—we might burst open. Renewal is not a mental thing; it is the revival of our heartfelt energy. To revive your enthusiasm, you need an inner-outer connection. You ask inside, through prayer, and you act outside to demonstrate that you are open. The universe will match you at the point of action. When I have felt stagnation in my life, it has been the willingness to call forth assistance from the higher levels that have never failed to bring about the necessary shift. When we feel stuck, some part of our soul is knocking on our heart, asking to be called upon so it can help us transform our lives. Through prayer, we can bring about renewal and inspiration from within. As we pray with the intention of a shift, it is bound to happen. That heartfelt energy, connected to the spirit, is magical.

This is a prayer for anyone who might feel stuck in the routine of their lives and wishes instead to see each day as a new opportunity to reach in and reach out, to awaken deeper compassion in themselves, and find new ways to serve others—to change their lives by cultivating a creative and divine imagination.

There is always more love to discover, more petals to open in the flower of yourself. We are always in the process of evolving. Let us pray together with enthusiasm for renewal and forward movement in the new day.

The Prayer

Dear Beloved,

Today is not just another day that piles on from yesterday.

Today is a brand new day because I am breathing, I am alive, and I can tap into endless possibilities. How grand is that!

Just like the weather is never the same, things in nature are always changing, and everything is moving in the universe. I welcome this brand new day, and I ask that I may look at this day with brand new eyes, not assuming it will be like yesterday.

Revive my enthusiasm and let that spill over into everything I do without taking for granted the little miracles of life or forgetting to be grateful for every little thing—most of all, for the gift of my life.

Help me make this day a brand new day. No matter the circumstances of my life, let me find the newness in myself and break down the walls that I have built between me—my heart—and others.

Let me drop any judgments about how I think my life should be and embrace everything that is. From that place, let me make new choices that bring the spirit of more kindness, more tenderness, more love, and more laughter so that the spirit that makes all things move can also move in me and make this moment—and the next one, and the next, and the next—a brand new moment.

I turn my gaze inward so that I can see how I might have forgotten and been blinded to the miracle of life that surrounds me. I forgive myself for any judgments I have placed against myself, my life, the people who surround me, and the world, for the hardships and the challenges I face, and for life not giving me what I want. I forgive myself for thinking that I have been denied or left behind. Whatever voice inside of me that has been undermining me and whispering fear and self-doubt into my ears, I now silence it. Allow me to see the truth of who I am and not the habit of who I have become.

Help me trust that I am one breath away from knowing that the conditions of my life can be transformed with the power of the spirit to experience more grace, more ease, more loving, and yes, more joy.

I dare to let my heart soften and open up to love.
So be it.

Prayer for Self-Expression

Dear Beloved,

I ask that I may open my eyes and see the infinite possibilities that exist, and that I may see the stream of creativity that exists in me.

Is there a way for me to open my heart, my vision, and my eyes so I may see myself through the eyes of my maker? So that I may receive a greater amplifier of my voice? So that my voice can come out and be expressed in creative ways? So that all that is in me can be birthed and find fertile ground to grow? So that I may feel the joy and happiness of my becoming?

I ask with all my heart to be willing to let go of the limited way I see myself, and be shown the ways that are there for me, though they are unknown to me at this moment. I ask to be willing to trust and know that I matter, and what I have to say also matters.

Tonight, as I sleep, I ask that my unconscious and my subconscious mind release the limitation, judgment, and resistance so that I may open up to the great consciousness of the divine and the higher intelligence that is part of me— so that I might start to embody, see, believe, breathe in, and manifest who I am meant to become.

So be it.

11

Hearing the Whisper of Your Creativity

When I was writing my third book, *Unbinding the Heart,* I intended to tell the story of how I discovered the gift of my expression. But in starting to write it, I was daunted by the fact that I was going to share my very profound inner experiences. Would I find the right words to communicate them?

When I started writing, everything was raw and written in stream of consciousness, and I often found myself sharing stories that seemed insignificant at the time. But an inner voice would whisper, "Don't judge it; just write it." As I started to trust that inner voice, I felt a release, as if the river dam was opened, and the words poured out of me. I trusted my creative flow and where it would lead me. Little by little, the stories emerged, the pivotal points of my life were shared, and I was delighted to find that there was more there than I could have imagined.

It was an extraordinary gift to discover that my creativity had lain dormant until I had the courage to tell my stories and reveal my inner world. I believe that all of us have creativity within us, we just need the courage to express it, whether on paper, in painting, in dance or song, through gardening or cooking or any type of creation. However, many of us feel afraid of exploring our own creativity, especially in the beginning.

When we first begin to express our creativity, we feel like children who are learning to walk; there are many times we fall and stumble. The difference between us and children is that children never judge themselves. They don't have the critical voice. A child stands and falls, and then gets up and knows somehow that they are going to walk. They are meant to walk. The impulse is embedded in a child's body.

It's the same with creativity; it is embedded in us, but our adult mind judges it. We come up with a thousand what-ifs: What if it's not good enough? What if people don't like it? What if I'm rejected and not received by others? So we might as well not even try. We keep our gifts from the world because of this voice that doesn't allow us to, as choreographer Martha Graham would say, "Keep the channel open."

It's a funny thing about our ego: it will stop us from moving forward because it does not want our image to be cracked. It's trying to keep us safe, and there is nothing safe about creativity. When we create, we enter unknown territories that form as we go along. In a way, we have to cede control over what the result will be; we have to be willing to attempt something, and if we don't like the outcome, start again. We must risk looking foolish and awkward, and most of all, we must suspend all judgments. We must surrender to what ultimately is the divine joy of our creativity. But you can't get there by thinking about it or analyzing it; you get there by rolling up your sleeves and diving in.

Take a moment to go into your place of quiet and ask yourself: What is it that I've wanted to create? Get this image in your mind's eye and bring it forth in its own dynamic imagery. What would it look like? What would it feel like? What would it make you feel when you put it together? What would it feel like to birth that idea? Make your vision as specific and as alive as possible and bring it into the present moment, and then, little by little, keep taking the next steps to manifest your creative expression, and ask, with all your heart, for support from the spirit that knows you and loves you and wants you to create.

Have fun with it. Make it a happy experience. Whatever project it is that you're starting, be careful not to fall into the trap of discouragement. You will run into stumbling blocks, or you may have a dry spell and won't know what to do next—that's okay! That's all part of the process.

Remember that your creative expression, in any form, is a gift, and you have a responsibility to nurture it, fertilize it, and tend to it, just as you would tend to a garden—weeding out the judgments, comparisons, and thoughts of unworthiness and self-doubt.

Opening up to your creativity is a form of prayer. You allow yourself to go beyond your personality, your ego, and your judgments and crack the door open to your soul.

So go for it! What do you have to lose other than maybe a protected self-image? Do you want to go through your life living in this limited image, or do you want to find the expanded version of yourself? The expanded version of yourself meets you when you dare to open the door.

The Prayer

Dear Beloved,

I ask now that I may allow my expression to flow freely.
I ask that I may trust myself to bring forth whatever I hear inside, to follow my creative pulse, to withhold

nothing, and to trust that I will be given the guidance to bring forth what is mine to bring forth.

I ask to suspend all judgments and all criticisms, and not second guess myself—to allow my process.

I give myself permission to not know the whole picture or the whole outcome. I give myself permission to take every step as it is present in the day, and to trust that the pieces will unfold and will be revealed to me.

I ask that I may be connected to my source, know that I am a creative being, and not compare my expression to anyone else's.

I may receive inspiration from others, and I may see others' extraordinary expressions, but that does not mean that mine aren't as good.

I ask that I may know the depths of my being, that I am a creator, that I am part of the creator, and therefore, I, too, have been given the gift to create. It is my God-given gift.

I release myself from any self-imposed pressure and I allow my own rhythm to unfold. I do this as an offering back to the life that is given to me and to the uniqueness that is mine to live by.

I allow divine inspiration. No matter how small my contribution is, I do not judge it as insignificant because in every garden and in every orchard, it's the tiny little flowers that make up the whole.

I am excited to see what unfolds and experience the gift of my creativity.

So be it.

~~~~~~

Quick God Fix to Lift the Spirit in a Challenging Meeting

I ask that the spirit oversee this meeting and lift the energy of stagnation and separation in order to open the gates of communication.

~~~~~~

12

Asking God to Come with Me to My Job Interview

*. . . when you have a dream, it doesn't often come at you screaming
in your face. . . . Sometimes a dream almost whispers. . . .
And if you can listen to the whisper, and if it tickles your heart,
and is something you think you want to do for the rest of your life,
then that is going to be what you do for the rest of your life and
we will benefit from everything you do.*
—STEVEN SPIELBERG

My friend and I were having lunch, and she shared with me that
she had an interview the next day for what she thought was her
dream job. She had been looking for a job for a while, and she
was agonizing about how she should act and what she should

wear, writing out a script for how it would go. But she was setting herself up for a huge disappointment because she was missing the major puzzle piece: confidence in herself and her credentials. She was desperate, and if she didn't get the job, she would feel devastated. Right then and there, in the middle of the restaurant, I said, "Why don't we just pray about it so that you can feel the spirit leading the way to see if this is for you?" So, we prayed.

We prayed for her to feel empowered, knowing that she had the qualifications for this job, but also to allow herself to be present and dynamic during the interview instead of having everything rehearsed in her head. We prayed for her to know that there are many opportunities, so she could trust that this was not the only one. Afterward, she said to me, "I feel like I'm exhaling." She was holding on to so much pressure, and I knew if we hadn't prayed, she would have walked into the interview with all that extra baggage. Through prayer, she allowed herself to open up to a greater level of trust, knowing that if this was meant for her, she would get it.

The feeling of wanting something often puts us in a scarcity mindset. We have a sense that we are lacking in whatever it is we want, and this often pushes away what we want. This robs us of the feeling of wholeness that is our birthright. Of course, we all want different things at different times. There is nothing wrong with wanting! But we approach it with the wrong mindset. If we trust that the universe will provide what we want instead of fearing that the universe will deny us, we are able to bring a sense of abundance into our lives.

My friend called me after the interview and said she felt amazing. She felt a sense of joy and connection with the people there, and she had never felt so free and trusting. It took a while for them to respond to her, and in this waiting time she focused on letting go of her desire for the job. She went on other interviews, and then let go, and then wanted the job again. About a month later, they called and offered her the job. Her real victory, however, was that she presented the fullness of herself during the interview.

Two of my friends are in public relations and marketing, each equally talented, equally wonderful. One of them is always struggling to get clients, and when she gets them, they never pay her enough, they're not nice people, and they get into conflicts with her. She is overworked and underpaid. My other friend has people knocking at her door. She's very successful and well known in her field, and everyone wants her to represent them. When I look at those two people, there's no inherent reason why one is incredibly successful and the other is always struggling. The difference is that one has a limiting belief that undermines her success. She believes that everything is hard and that she never gets rewarded. The other has tremendous confidence in herself and a lot of chutzpah, and she is able to promote herself without any mental blocks.

As you pursue your dreams, ask yourself: What is my underlying belief about the jobs I want and the opportunities I want to create? Do I believe that I deserve to be supported? Often, if our parents and teachers never really believed in us or encouraged us, it takes a lot of chiseling away to find out why you are not giving yourself permission to have the success you deserve. Once you clear the cobwebs, fields of opportunities will open for you.

Make it a habit to tap into your infinite supply, which is the divine source that gives us life. If you learn to connect with that power, people are bound to resonate with you. In your attempts to get what you want, assume the feeling that it is already yours to have. Sometimes you have to fake it till you make it. You might not feel it all the way, but if you are feeling paralyzed with need, other people will sense it and respond negatively toward you. The more you make God your partner—which is my favorite affirmation ever—and the more you anchor that in your very cells and become a vortex or magnet of the good coming to you, the more the universe will respond to you. The opportunities will find you.

The Prayer

Dear Beloved,

I ask of the spirit that wants the best for me to connect with the part that is fearful, doubtful, and apprehensive about the upcoming job interview.

I ask that I may know my value and ability to do well at this job I am interviewing for. As I go into this interview, I trust that I don't walk alone, but instead I walk with the spirit that opens doors for me.

If this opportunity is meant for me and my highest good, and will enhance my life's fulfillment, I ask that I receive this job. If this isn't for me and my highest good, I ask that I may let it go and trust that my opportunity will come in perfect timing.

As I walk into this interview, I have a sense of confidence and a sense of myself, and no feeling that this is the be-all and end-all. My wisdom carries me forward and shows me the way.

Most of all, I see the light in me shine. I feel my joy, I smile, and I connect with my inner authority in who I am as I go out into the world. I leave the rest to God.

So be it!

Prayer for When You're Broke

If your cellar is empty,
This whole universe
Could drink forever from mine!
—HAFIZ

Dear Beloved,

I feel like I am in the desert, and wherever I look, I see dry land. I have no idea how to come out of this barren place that I am in.

I quiet myself. I bow down to your assistance that must be somewhere, since I am still breathing. What is it that I have done to make myself feel so dried out, in matters of money, relationships, creativity, or purpose?

I am willing to have a shift in my mind and heart. I hear the voice of my wisdom, asking me to let go of judgment, bitterness, or feelings of being wrong in some way.

Now, I breathe in the forgiveness. I breathe in forgiveness even more deeply. I surrender. I stop blaming myself and life, as if I am neglected or abandoned, and I return, to the best of my ability, to filling myself up again with the joy of my life force.

I see myself being lifted out of the desert, as if a parachute were lifting me off the ground and carrying me to a garden. In that garden, I allow myself to open the gate and look at the abundance of the fertile ground, the flowers, the trees, the ponds, and the river streams, and feel the breeze of your embrace.

I let myself exhale. I let myself smile. For the first time in a long time, I trust that I have resources and that resources will come to me. As I enjoy myself and bask in the beauty of this garden, with so much growth and nature all around me, I allow myself to see that, if this is possible in nature, it is possible in my life, since I am also part of this creation.

I see opportunities where I thought there were none. I see the miracle of support and assistance and people who come to my aid. I allow this new receptivity to inhabit me.

I take my right hand and place it on my heart. I take my left hand and place it on my belly. I connect the part of me that has felt alone, insecure, and deprived with the openness of my heart that is connected directly to you, directly to my higher self, directly to my source. I send messages to my emotional self that I am not alone, I have done nothing wrong, I am loved, I am guided, and I have the strength and the courage to take the next steps forward in my life.

I will return to this place often and remember that, at any point, if I find myself in the desert, I can be lifted into the garden—because I am willing, I am willing, I am willing to see with new eyes the blessings that life can provide me.

So be it.

PS: Please nudge me when I forget!

13

You Hold the Keys to Your Purpose

My heart is at ease knowing that what was meant for me will never
miss me, and what misses me was never meant for me.
—Imam Al-Shafi'i

I often encounter people who don't know what their purpose is. Especially when we are young, we try to make sense of our world, build a career, and find fulfillment in our lives. But it is common for people who have very successful careers to still feel unfulfilled and disconnected.

There is a distinction between what you do and what your purpose is. I believe every person has one purpose while on this earth: to awaken to who they truly are, find their gifts, and serve other human beings with them. Your purpose is nothing grandiose or glamorous and has nothing to do with feeling recognized or validated. When you find your purpose, you feel at peace; no matter what happens in life, you have a sense of rootedness and connection.

In this chapter, I want to speak especially to younger people who struggle with two competing drives: to find work that will bring success, and to engage with and contribute to a community.

Ask yourself often: What am I here to learn? What am I here to teach? What am I here to overcome? What am I here to complete? What am I here to express or to share? Am I enjoying my life, and if not now, when?

This is when prayer can be so beneficial to you, because prayer connects you to your higher self, which can reveal your purpose and your calling *to you*. Through prayer, you can find fulfillment while you are in the process of unfolding. You will find that these questions will allow you to function from a place of learning, sharing, and teaching, and you'll start feeling much more purposeful by doing all the little things that contribute to a bigger vision of yourself. Even if you aren't where you want to be in your career, staying focused on these questions will center you in the process of finding your purpose. It's a learning process. It expands you, and asking these questions in prayer will allow you to see your life in a much fuller way.

You might not hear a direct answer to these questions, but be patient in your quiet reflection. When we bow in prayer and enter a state of reverence, we connect with the presence of God in us. In doing so, we start to experience a sense of purpose. We become human beings rather than human doings. Then, it doesn't matter what you do, because whatever you do, you will do from that place of connection. Even if you are simply washing the car or baking a pie, you will feel a sense of purpose because you are alive within yourself.

For a long time, I thought that my acting career was my purpose, and because it wasn't flourishing for many years, I felt purposeless. I had to dig deeper and discover that what I really wanted was the ability to freely express myself. So as I embarked on a deeper exploration of myself through studying psychology and spirituality, I started to better know myself and the spirit within me, and I started pursuing projects that allowed me to fully express my creativity. Instead of relying on the world to give me what I wanted, I became proactive in giving the world what I had inside of me. That was the biggest shift in my mindset; I was no longer dependent on the external world accepting me and giving me the roles I wanted. I became my own creative source.

In order to do that, I had to find out what I had to offer. I think the trap that a lot of us fall into is that we wait for the world to give us permission to make an entrance. We wait for something to happen in the world because we don't really trust that we have it inside of us. In my experience, it took guts and prayer and listening to push myself off the diving board. I had to find the still place inside of me as a source of steadiness amidst the restlessness of the question of my purpose. There were many times when I was getting ready to perform that I would shake and feel tremendous trepidation: What if I fail? What if I have nothing to say? What if this project collapses? But I had to keep moving past my negative fears and doubts. Shakespeare said it best: "Our doubts are traitors, and make us lose the good we oft might win, by fearing to attempt."

Sometimes, when the universe doesn't give us what we think we want, it instead offers us the greatest gift: forcing us to look within and realize that what we truly want is ourselves. This was my experience. I didn't get the acting roles, but I got Agapi: the opportunity to play myself fully on the greater stage of the world.

The Prayer

Dear Beloved,

Thank you for this moment. Thank you for being there and shining a light on me, my life, and my purpose.

As I am embarking on this journey of my work, my life, and my relationships, I ask that I receive assistance to understand what I am here to do on this earth.

When I feel alone and disconnected in the world, please show me that I am always connected to you. I open myself to this shift in my awareness. I ask that I may know that I was born with a purpose embedded in my heart, so that I may experience love, express my creativity, feel connected to myself and others, and know joy.

I open the gates for you to show me the purpose in my everyday life.

Allow me to experience who I am.

Allow me to see that my purpose doesn't have to come with fanfare; it can gently glide into my heart and give me peace of mind and a steadiness of direction that will capture my heart and bring me a sense of calm. Let me hear the whisper in my ear that I am here for a reason. I came to learn, grow, share, give, receive, and experience. This, I know.

How wondrous it is to fill the empty spaces with your love, trusting that I will find the courage and feel the confidence that I never walk alone.

So be it.

~~~~~~~~~~~~~~~~~~~~~~~~

Quick God Fix to Have More Fun

Ignite my magic that can transform the moment and allow me to laugh, dance, and sing again.

~~~~~~~~~~~~~~~~~~~~~~~~

Prayer for When You're Feeling Burnt Out

Dear Beloved,

I have been going nonstop. I have lost my boundaries, and I feel I am about to lose myself in the burden of my work. I have lost my enjoyment and my creativity. I feel as though I am on a treadmill and I can't get off.

Please assist me in knowing how to back away so that I may return to a sense of inner connection, regain the ability to delegate and set limits on what I am able to contribute, and release any judgment of myself. I ask also that I may be *given the wisdom and guidance to know whether it may be time to change jobs or take a break. Can I afford to take a break?*

I quiet myself and listen for guidance, but most of all, I want to hear the loving voice in my heart that tells me it is okay to rest, that it is okay to step back.

I have so overidentified with my work that I am afraid that, if I let go, I will also lose my identity. Please let me feel your loving arms around me. Maybe I need to cry, to release the pressure that is put upon me and that I put upon myself. Once I release, I can exhale and remember to trust the bigger picture of my life.

Please send the light to any support from friends or colleagues who might come to me and show me there is a way—that I can shift my hours or my responsibilities while still producing and contributing.

I ask for the divine to show me the infinite solutions and possibilities before me and release any burdens in my heart.

So be it.

III

Becoming

14

Becoming You: The Greatest Accomplishment

During a podcast interview, the host asked me a great question: "How did you become you?" I was taken aback by the profundity of that question. The becoming of oneself never really ends and is constantly unfolding and expanding, but there was a definite moment in my life when I embarked on my journey.

I was in London and had graduated from drama school; I was living with my mother and sister, Arianna, and feeling insecure and overwhelmed by the unknowns of my life. I didn't know how to pursue a career, how to start working as an actress, or how to decide if I should go back to Greece to be with my father and friends. My sister had traveled to Los Angeles to promote a book she had written about the feminist movement, titled *The Female Woman*. There, she had met a wonderful Greek man who financed movies. They struck up a friendship, and Arianna told him about my dream of acting. He offered to invite me to come to Los Angeles and audition for a movie he was producing.

Sure enough, a few weeks later I was sent an airline ticket to Los Angeles to audition for the movie. I was elated with the sense that my destiny was about to unfold. I felt this incredible energy of hope and fearlessness as I was embarking on entirely unknown territory. The rest of the story reads like a Hollywood film. I was flown first-class, picked up in a limo, and put up at the Beverly Hills Hotel. I was introduced to Arianna's friend, the movie producer and my Greek benefactor, and I met the director. I auditioned for the movie, and the audition went well. The director told me I would be perfect for the part, and they would let me know when the movie was green-lit. I felt optimistic, that something good was going to happen. My life began filling up with new introductions, endless meetings, and social gatherings, and I was so well taken care of that I began to feel at home in Los Angeles. But I hadn't heard anything about the movie.

Eventually, I got a call from my Greek benefactor. I thought he was going to tell me the good news: we were finally going to start production on the movie. Instead, he told me, "Agapi, I am sorry to tell you that the financing didn't come through, and we're not going to be moving forward with the movie, but I have your return ticket to London, so let me know what date you would like to depart." I was completely stunned. I felt like the rug had been pulled out from under my feet. I could barely respond. I remember saying, "Thank you, Nick. Let me think about what I'm going to do."

A few days later, I was sitting in my hotel room staring at my return ticket on the table, and there was nothing in me that wanted to use it. It just wasn't happening. I felt as if I was staring into the abyss of the unknown, but with a deep knowing that I had to find the courage to stay the course. When I thought of returning to London, it seemed that there was nothing to go back to. My inner knowing was that I needed to stay in Los Angeles and trust that things would work out. It's a funny thing about big life decisions that we make. Maybe part of us is scared, but another part of us has the blueprint of our lives and is guiding us and pushing us to make the choice that is right for our growth and evolution. Although we don't have the script for what our life is going to look like, we have the thread that connects us to our inner knowing that is ever so powerful and is always with us. Every human being has that blueprint within them. We are always connected and guided, but we must take the time to listen, to ask, and to trust. The invisible light of our soul and our inner path requires that we listen beyond what we can hear, and imagine beyond what we can see, so that we can put the pieces of our lives, one by one, into place until we reveal the puzzle in its entirety.

I decided to stay in Los Angeles. God knows how I was going to make it because I had no income, no job, and no prospects for work because I didn't have a green card. But I had tons of friends who opened their homes and hearts to me. After all, being born in Greece, one of the things I was raised with was an ability to bond with people, open my heart, and share. Sure enough, generosity was something I was always met with in my life. I embarked on my quest even though I didn't yet know what I was searching for. I didn't believe in God at that point, or in anything beyond myself. But I did start to follow a yoga practice in Los Angeles, and I connected with the teacher. He knew I had no income but saw my devotion to and incredible love for yoga, and he said to me, "Please come to my classes as my guest." *Autobiography of a Yogi* by Paramahansa Yogananda was for sale at the reception desk, which was the book that my mother kept by her bedside in Greece when I was a young girl. As you might recall, this would be the book that would set me on the path to my spiritual awakening. My choice to stay in Los Angeles was spirit-led.

During that time, I prayed for a teacher because I knew I needed a guide. A friend from London who was in Los Angeles called and invited me to a retreat in Malibu with a teacher named Swami Muktananda, who was very well-known in the spiritual community. I asked to meet Swami privately, and while sitting beside a big tree, I told him of my experience of spiritual awakening. He said to me, "You are very blessed. Your deep desire to wake up woke you up, where most people need a teacher to support their awakening. I am not your teacher, there is someone else that waits for you." "Wow," I thought. "How does he know that, and how am I going to find them?"

Soon after, I connected with a beautiful actor who told me she was studying with a Western teacher named John-Roger, and she invited me to a seminar he was leading. When I heard his name, something inside of me lit up. A week later, I went with my new friend to the ashram where John-Roger was speaking. I walked in, and he walked toward me and said, "You are Agapi; welcome home." That was it. I found my teacher. I found my path. I've never looked back or second-guessed that this was where I belonged. It was my destiny being fulfilled, and I can truly say, since then, everything in my life has been divinely guided.

I took many classes and seminars, and I proceeded with a passion to embark on this spiritual path, open my heart to more healing and loving, and evolve. The way I see it, life gave us life, and we are part of life. We are not randomly thrown onto this earth to figure it out on our own. We have the solutions embedded and embroidered inside of us, but we must walk every step of the way. The events of our lives—the hard ones, the difficult ones—are all part of the teaching. Becoming yourself is not a linear path. It's personal and unique to each one of us. But the journey inward, with all the peaks and valleys it entails, is worth all the effort we can devote to it; none of it is wasted as long as we keep returning to our true home within ourselves.

The Prayer

Dear Beloved,

I ask for the light to help me transform every day of my life. I ask to be able to understand that every day, every event, and everything that does and doesn't happen to me is part of my understanding of the soul of who I am, the being of who I am, and the joy of who I am.

I ask that the parts of me that doubt, that feel a sense of hopelessness or despair, be transmuted into the light, and in their place I ask to find joy, hope, love, and expansion. Even in my most uncertain moments, I ask to know that I am taken care of and there is a path carved out for me even if I can't see it.

I ask that love be embedded in my heart, mind, and self because I am love made manifest. My very cells right now are kept alive and together by the vibration and consciousness of love.

I am so grateful to know the light. I am so grateful to know that there is more to me than this physical body and the reality of my life. Whatever parts of me don't know this, please allow me to see them.

I am open, I receive, and I celebrate the miracle of my life as I watch myself become.

So be it!

A Short Blessing for You

May you know you are blessed
May you know you are loved
May you walk in peace
May you let yourself be led by the one who knows
    the way
May you sing your song
May you know your value beyond this world
May you utter the words of your unspoken truth
May you dare say no to that which is not for you
May you dare say yes when you hear the calling

May you care for yourself like you care for others
May you grieve your losses and rejoice in your new
discoveries
May you write your story
May you share your wisdom
May you know the art of letting go and the art of
knowing what belongs to you and what belongs to
others
May you know your center and come to it every day, and
build your house there so that it never shakes or
feels the quakes of life
May you walk in peace and see the view from all
perspectives, and let the wind touch your spirit and
carry it into the world
May you know your heart, its beauty, and its vastness
May you know yourself and God's immensity in you.

15

The God Diet

I ran into a friend of mine after having not seen her for a year, and she had lost over seventy pounds; she looked amazing! And I asked her, "How did you do it?" and she said, "God." I said, "Yes, but how did you *really* do it?" She smiled and repeated, "God!"

She explained that she prayed to find the right approach to weight loss, and then she discovered a plan through which she was able to lose weight in a way that was sustainable without making her feel deprived. Her experience with weight loss seemed to be full of grace. I think everyone, in some way or another, struggles with their relationship with food. Food is so much more than just nutrition. It fills emotional voids, is an amazing coping mechanism, becomes a source of comfort, and can also be an enemy. Food is such a big part of our lives.

Establishing a joyful relationship with food is a healthy foundation for your well-being. Growing up in Greece, food was an essential part of my culture. Greeks celebrate life through food. If you go out with a group of friends, there is always going to be an abundance of food to be shared. Every meeting, celebration, and gathering is centered around food. My mother was obsessed with food. She loved shopping at the supermarket, cooking, and serving everyone who came to our home, including the FedEx delivery person. My mother would invite them in for a cup of soup, a cookie, a sandwich, or a Greek dessert. If we had people over for dinner, everyone left with a goody bag. Feeding people was her way of showing she cared.

As a little girl, I was extremely thin. My appetite was suppressed. I was internalizing the turmoil my parents were going through—I had much anxiety and felt unsafe around my father's erratic moods—and it diminished my desire for food. As I grew older and left to study in England, my relationship with food became healthier. I loved and enjoyed my thin body until many years later, when my metabolism started to change and I gradually put on weight.

I embarked on every diet imaginable to the point of starvation. Every time I lost the excess weight, I felt amazing! But, without fail, the fifteen to twenty pounds would come right back. At some point, I hit menopause, and it took over my body. There was very little I could control about it. It takes such discipline and willpower to stay vigilant about our choices around food: eating at the right times, exercising, and watching calories. With my Greek genetics, my body completely changed, and I had to accept it and learn to love myself regardless. By that time, I had enough wisdom to know that my self-identity and my self-worth did not depend on my physical appearance. Who I am, what I contribute to the world, and how I feel about myself are far more meaningful than whether or not I am carrying extra pounds. I wanted to lose weight, but I gave it up. It was too much to deal with.

Years later, when I heard my friend's story, I was guided to pray about my own relationship to food. When I invited in the wisdom of my higher self, I became aware that some part of me was holding on to extra weight because that extra weight made me feel safe, grounded, and protected. I was reluctant to let it go. As I brought the spirit forward in prayer, I, too, started to release the excess weight I had been carrying. My relationship with food began to change because I felt more trusting of myself, more secure in myself, and more at home in my body. I looked at the patterns that were keeping me from sticking to a program. I also looked at my habitual tendency to use food for comfort.

For example, why was it that every night—because I stay up late at night—I would go to the refrigerator to find a little treat? A piece of chocolate, a cracker, or some cheese. I realized that this unconscious pattern was due to some part of me that was looking for nourishment at night—an emotional outlet, entertainment, connection. It was a very old pattern because it was based on a very old fear that I needed to soothe within myself. Whatever restlessness was going on in my unconscious needed to be quieted and numbed before I could fall asleep. This clarity allowed me to release this unconscious habit and move into greater alignment with food.

My late night snacking stopped, and I was able to release about fifteen pounds. It seemed easy, even effortless, like there was an inner cooperation. The joy of returning to the leaner version of myself was exhilarating. I found foods that really supported me, and I had fewer cravings for breads, sweets, and carbohydrates in general. We all know the struggle of wanting foods that we know are not the best choices for our health. Somehow that struggle subsided in me. I've found success with intermittent fasting, in which you don't eat for sixteen hours, between the last meal in the evening and the first meal in the morning. There is a tremendous amount of science that tells us how good it is for the body to rest and recharge between meals so it can regenerate. I was never a morning eater anyway, so that really works for me.

I know how I want to feel in my body—vital and energized—which is connected to how I eat. If I'm considering eating granola that has brown sugar and maple syrup on it, I know that as appetizing as it looks, my energy will drop after eating it. On the other hand, a smoothie with macadamia nut milk, almond butter, collagen, and hemp will give me long-term satisfaction. With prayer, I have opened my heart to myself and become more compassionate with myself. I am gentler with myself, and I let go of the pressure and the judgment. My choices around food are no longer a struggle but rather a process of self-discovery.

I'm sharing these small details with you because I feel we all can have a very healthy, joyful relationship with food, but it takes getting down to what the real issues are, educating ourselves, and praying for the answers. We have to ask ourselves some basic questions: Am I judging my body? Do I have an image of myself that I'm not meeting? Am I beating myself up because of it?

Whatever your situation is, whatever your judgment is, it's imperative that you let go of any shame that you have about your body. It doesn't matter if someone is seen as overweight or the perfect size; shame stays inside the body in a very deep place. In this prayer, I want to bring in the spirit to unravel our unconscious and infuse the food we eat with joy and celebration. It's a wonderful thing to have an appetite and enjoy the many delicious things there are to eat in this world. As we eat these foods, remember that nourishment is one of the most loving things we can do for ourselves.

The Prayer

Dear Beloved,

I ask now that I let you into my life and my thoughts around food. I let you in to what I eat, when I eat, and how I eat, and ask you to help me embrace food as a nurturing and nourishing element in my life.

Whatever issue I'm struggling with, let me first ask for your assistance in knowing that food is completely and directly related to my health. If I have any judgments of my body—whether my body is overweight, underweight, or even at the perfect weight—let me release those judgments and instead look at my body as a miraculous instrument of life that I have a responsibility to honor, protect, and care for.

My body has been bestowed upon me and is the carrier of my soul's energy, so assist me in elevating my attitude toward my body and not taking it for granted.

I ask now that I may have assistance in releasing the shame, if there is any shame, around my body.

Show me a picture of myself in radiant health, at the size and fitness level that is right for me. Remind me that my body is a miracle made from thirty-seven trillion cells; my body is the miracle of life.

My organs, my blood, my veins, my bones, my muscles, my vocal cords, my brain, my extraordinary heart that beats, my very breath is the spirit of life and the spirit of God in me. So who am I to judge, criticize, withhold, punish, or reject any parts of me?

I ask to forgive myself for thinking I am not good enough in my body because it might be overweight, underweight, not fit enough, or lazy, for wanting to have more to eat when I know I'm full, or for always using food to find support, security, and comfort.

Let me find comfort in you, in the love for myself, and know that everything I eat is blessed to become nutrients for this miracle of life.

Let me eat the things that have vital energy, sustain me, and improve my health. Let me become a student of my body so that I may find which foods support and energize me. Let me rediscover the magic of food, the magic of nutrition, and the magic of feeding myself. Let me take a moment before I eat to bless the food before me.

All I ask for now is to redefine my relationship with food, not from a place of restriction and deprivation, but from a vision of the healthiest version of myself.

Most of all, know that I invite you in now to show me the best path for me—the people who can support me, like nutritionists, doctors, and friends—so whatever I decide to do will come from a place of caring and devotion.

I bless my process. I bless my food. I become present and mindful with myself as I eat, and I take my caring spirit with me in my journey through a new love affair with food for my health and my well-being.

So be it.

16

The Hidden Gifts of Being Alone

I have encountered loneliness many times on my journey. My joy and connection come through my family, friends, and engagement in many different life experiences. I feel more alive when I interact with people whom I love. My heart opens up and is filled with my own joy in other people's uniqueness; when alone, this energy seems to diminish. I am a classic extrovert!

I was talking with one of my dearest friends and said, "I am so lonely." And she said, "How can you be lonely? You are with one of my favorite people in the world!" I needed to become my own favorite person in the world.

In Greece, we would never go to the movies or dinner or an outing on our own; we always went with someone else or in groups. I maintained that habit for many years. If I dared go to a movie on my own, I thought that everyone was looking at me. Well, of course, nobody cared, and over the years I learned to love my own company. Eventually, I was able to go out to lunch or sit at a café alone. I felt I was taking myself out. I started to enjoy going to the movies, shopping, and taking long walks with my thoughts alone, just being with me. We all must make peace with the fact that no matter who we are with, we are always with ourselves. We come into this world with ourselves, and we die with ourselves. If we build a deeper love and connection with ourselves, we can enjoy a richer life, have greater God-filled days while on this earth, and ultimately have more fun.

It took a lot of inner work to experience my own fullness in the absence of others. When I would meditate and disconnect from the world to go to deeper parts of myself, I felt connected, but after coming out of the meditation, I felt a block between the spiritual inner world and the outer material world. I needed to build a stronger bridge between my spiritual self and my worldly self. I had been interfering with the flow of the spirit by judging myself and others and demanding more from life than what was possible, which created feelings of lack within me. These are the products of the false self or, as I call them, my children of darkness. If we are able to move beyond these negative patterns of thinking and feeling, we will always be connected to the universal consciousness. It takes a willingness to see ourselves through the spiritual lens, but if we can, there is no way we will feel lonely.

We are all conditioned to be oriented outward, to look for fulfillment and connection out in the world, but in doing so we leave the treasures of who we are behind. As a result, we feel a void within us that cannot be filled by anything external. In my life journey, I did not get many things I believed I wanted, like a successful acting career, a fulfilling relationship with a man, and various creative projects that I tried to develop that didn't materialize. Now, looking back, I can see that this was all a setup by my soul to lead me back to my true self.

I took full responsibility for my happiness and stopped waiting for something to happen in order for me to be happy. That's when I felt empowered—by knowing that I was the source of my loneliness and also the source of my happiness. Ultimately, I think that is what we're all seeking: to feel alive and full in who we are, which is richer than anything we can conceive. But the world never teaches us how to get there. Everything on this plane of existence is designed to make us forget who we are. So my prayer for each one of us is that we will re-remember who we are beyond our conditioned and limited senses of ourselves that make us believe we are not enough. Remember, you are nothing less than divine.

I was once on an island in Greece, looking out over the Aegean Sea, when I felt a sense of home within myself, and I was moved to write this poem:

~~~~~~

Coming Home

I used to be so lonely
lonely at my house
lonely when I got back to sleep
lonely when I was alone.
When I was with people
I was never lonely
but when by myself loneliness would hit my home
And then one day I heard a voice
Why don't you move in
I live alone too
You would like it here
Move in with me
I looked around and it was me talking to me
My house was empty
Wow, I said
I left that beautiful place a long time ago

Going out looking for others to fill my home
    and I left my house empty
Move in move in with me
You'll like it here
You'll never have to pay rent
I'll never evict you
You'll be my honored guest
I know you
Your likes your dislikes your little quintessential
    idiosyncrasies
I know You
I will treat you nice and kind and give you lots of space
Move in, come, move in with me
I looked into my eyes, my heart,
And saw the love for me
I surrendered, I opened the door and moved in
Into my empty house that
I had left a long time ago
It was exactly as I left it
It had just missed me
I moved in and never left
And never felt alone anymore
For my house filled with love once I accepted such a
    kind invitation.

The Prayer

Dear Beloved,

I ask for the warmth of the light and the presence of the spirit to envelop, protect, and surround all parts of myself.

I ask that any separation between me and myself be healed and that I might create a loving environment within myself so any parts of me that feel neglected or not good enough will be given expression.

I ask that I connect with my inner guidance, my higher self, and the invisible support that is available to assist me.

I ask that I may reveal to myself the beauty and the riches of my inner world, which can transform my loneliness into the joy of being alone.

Let me be the most gracious host to all parts of myself, even the darkness, the jealousy, the feelings of inadequacy, and the vulnerable aspects of myself that feel so human.

Please help me remove the obstacles to being there for myself.

Let me smile from within as I hear the whisper of the Beloved that says, "Don't you see my secret smile to remind you who you belong to? You belong to you; you belong to the Beloved."

So be it.

17

Replace Your Addiction with God

I was thinking the other day about all the things we're addicted to in this physical manifestation of this world. You can become addicted to accumulating things, advancing your career, or finding romantic love. You can become addicted to food, alcohol, drugs, or television. You can become addicted to feeling "less than," living your whole life feeling second best. You can become addicted to your thoughts, your anxieties, or your worries. You can become addicted to always needing to be on your own or always needing to be with people. You can become addicted to feeling the burdens of the world, and think that if you keep doing, serving, and overextending yourself, you will alleviate the suffering, but instead you end up feeling depleted. You can become addicted to spending money or to fearing the loss of what you have, so you end up not spending anything or, when you do, grieving your loss.

One of my addictions was taking care of other people. Don't get me wrong, it's a wonderful quality to want to take care of other people, but when you start to take care of other people at the expense of yourself, it's not a good thing. I have seen so many people assign themselves the role of the caretaker and use this as an excuse to not take care of themselves. For me, the underlying issue was that taking care of people gave me a sense of being valued, needed, and purposeful. Behind all addictions are core issues of control and insecurity—not feeling connected or safe. Opening yourself up to seeing what your addiction is, loving yourself through its release, and asking for the higher power to help you navigate forgiveness is one of the greatest services you can do for yourself.

What are you addicted to? Dissecting your addictive patterns and separating yourself from them will give you distance so you can start, little by little, unbuttoning the straitjacket you wear. When those limiting energies of your addiction grab you, you are experiencing far less of who you are. Trace back to the beginning of the addictive behavior. Was it something specific that happened early in your life that led you to use this coping mechanism to fill the void? This information might be locked in your unconscious. For me, it started when my parents separated. I felt unsafe, and I thought that if I took care of my father, or other people who came into my life, then I would belong. You might want to ask yourself: When did I first become addicted to this external crutch to make me feel more connected, safe, comforted, or in control?

Exploring the territory of your addictions can be enlightening. You can begin to experience freedom, space, and expansion in your life. It's a slow process because you're not going to free yourself overnight. It's a process that requires listening with patience and love. What I want you to embrace in this prayer is a willingness to let go of what consciously or unconsciously has been plaguing you and preventing you from experiencing the sweetness and blissfulness of your soul. If I had a universal eraser, I would erase limitation from the human consciousness and instead infuse every human being with the deep awareness that they are a miracle of life. Join me in this prayer, and add your own words to ask for help in releasing yourself from your addictive patterns.

The Prayer

Dear Beloved,

I ask for the light of the spirit to shine on me so that I may start experiencing a deeper fullness and wholeness of myself.

In my human form, I tend to look outside of myself and am drawn to addictive patterns, but I yearn for a deeper connection to spirit, to God, and to love.

I only know and see myself through this material world, so I ask now to open my heart and my spirit to know and see myself in my divinity as I embrace my humanness in all its aspects.

I ask that I release any judgments of my addictive patterns and that I may allow my wisdom to show me how to let go and bring more love and acceptance to myself, and find other ways to nurture myself and feel connected.

I ask that the sense of self and connection that I get from my addiction be replaced with the love of the spirit.

Please guide me, as I am willing to release this pattern and the deeper unconscious impulses that make me do things that violate who I am. If there is anyone who can come to support me as a guide, coach, or friend, please point me to the right person, for I might need help to get out of this labyrinth.

I ask for patience to see myself through this and welcome support on every level.

So be it.

Prayer for Knowing the Miracle of Life

Dear Beloved,

I recall my birth and its pure manifestation of light in this world, and I reflect on how my spirit entered my body and gave me life—this little body of a tiny baby that had flesh, bones, blood, veins, eyes, ears, a mouth, a brain, a heart, ten fingers, and ten toes.

The first cry—what a miracle of life!

Then, I grew and wondered who knew the perfect way for me to grow.

Who knew my thirty-three vertebrae would grow in perfect measure so that I could walk, bend, and stretch?

Who gave me my two vocal cords that helped me utter words to others, and my amazing bones that grew so strong and helped me stand and support this person I became?

How about the perfect eardrums, the eye sockets, the corneas, irises, and veins? Or the perfect eyes that opened and saw the world?

And the strands of my hair—how did they grow?

My forehead, the bones that hold the brain?

How miraculously, exquisitely put together is my body!

Whoever designed this brilliant, awestruck instrument of my form surely did not implant a limitation on my thoughts or my feelings, to make me feel any less than this incredible perfection.

So whatever negative decisions and beliefs I made about myself and whatever seeds were planted to grow into weeds that eat away at the roots of my divinity, let these now be transformed into the knowledge of the exquisiteness of my being, which cannot be denied.

Let me find the courage to stand in the awesome awareness that I was made in God's image, for who else would have made this instrument of me, this symphony of me, that is composed in such perfection.

I am the beneficiary of all that. I am to enjoy all that! I am to guard it like the most caring and nurturing gardener. I ask that I may be restored to my wholeness.

I am willing to forgive those that implanted in me feelings of inadequacy, worry, uncertainty, and shame—

feelings of lack, guilt, and blame. I forgive my teachers and my parents, the world around me that made me believe I am anything less than I am. I bow to my existence, and I embrace it.

So be it!

18

The Imprisonment of Perfectionism

And every day, the world will drag you by the hand, yelling,
"This is important! And this is important! And this is important!
You need to worry about this! And this! And this!"
And each day, it's up to you to yank your hand back,
put it on your heart and say, "No. This is what's important."
—Iain Thomas

So many people struggle with the idea of perfectionism. We all have a utopian idea of how we want our lives to be. For some people, it shows up as making sure every detail is taken care of—being neat, dressing impeccably, and being overly cautious to avoid mistakes. For me, my idea of perfection is people being good to one another, getting along with one another, and living happily ever after in my ideal Greek village! As you can imagine, that kind of expectation often sets me up for disappointment; never wanting discord, conflict, or arguments is an impossible demand to make.

When I looked back on my life to find the source of this idea of perfectionism, I remembered that as a young girl, barely a teenager, I created a fictional character named Anna who could do no wrong. She was perfect. She would say the perfect things and act in the perfect manner; she knew exactly how to interact with boys, and she even ate all the right things. I see now that this was my way of trying to figure out how to exist in a world in which my parents were separated and in so much pain as a result. I felt such uncertainty in my life that I was extremely insecure and vulnerable. Anna was my little friend who always knew what to do, and I relied on her perfection for a sense of security.

Prayer has helped me to find my inner core, a sense of an inner Anna—not in striving to be perfect, but rather an internal and unconditional source of love, security, and acceptance, the beloved in me. When I feel constricted by the desire for things to be perfect, prayer allows a soulfulness to become present and soften the edges of my ego. I have expanded my sense of how things should be, according to my personal manifesto! I pray to see things more holistically, so I may be a conduit of a higher love and light for myself and others.

I remember a dear friend of mine who was a highly neurotic perfectionist in every single way—the kind of woman who had to hang her clothes in the same direction on the hangers. She said to me, "It took the birth of my child to throw away every idea of perfection. Raising him, every day my perfectionism crashed. In the eyes of that child, in his unbridled energy, I found perfect harmony in life's imperfections."

My greatest liberation in writing books was letting go of this idea of perfection because, in the writing process, nothing ever travels from inspiration to the page perfectly. We write, discard, edit, erase, and write more. Writing is an endless process, and it's not linear. It's a creative and messy art that is discovered as you go along. It's the same way in your life: constant readjusting, rerouting, making U-turns, hitting dead ends, and recalculating routes. Perfectionism is a pattern that sabotages creativity and prevents us from accepting reality as it is. Allow yourself the dignity of your imperfections as you are evolving. We are all works in progress, on our way to becoming the masterpieces of our perfect souls.

Perfectionism runs rampant in the arena of spirituality as

well. We assume that spiritual people do not get upset, jealous, or angry. When we step onto the spiritual path, we feel that we should be perfect. We force ourselves not to feel our real feelings, not to say the things we want to say. It's a powerful pressure we place on ourselves, which denies the true essence of who we are. If we restrict ourselves, we never really get to experience the magnificent joy of our spiritual nature.

One of the things that deters people from a spiritual life is the deep knowing that spirit can dismantle all the structures we rely on in our lives as they are: who we think we are, how we think things should be, and what form we think our lives should take. Spirituality is, ultimately, a surrender to that which has no form. This relinquishing of control can be scary and runs directly counter to perfectionism, which is all about control.

Be mindful of spiritual perfectionism because the fundamental truth of spirituality is an acceptance and a love for how things are. I experience spirit as unconditional love that transforms our lower selves and embraces everything, including everything we call imperfections. Spirit is the ultimate alchemist, turning metals into gold.

What would your life be like if you gave up your ideal of perfectionism, whatever it looks like for you? That, in essence, is liberation. So let us pray.

The Prayer

Dear Beloved,

I see how my desire for things to be perfect and harmonious is costing me my well-being, my freedom, and my peace. I recognize the deep fear within me that if I let go, relax, and let things be as they are—sometimes messy and unpredictable, as life mostly is—everything will fall apart, including me.

I understand that my perfectionism was born out of a need for survival at a certain time in my life, when I believed that if I was perfect, I could control a world that, in my childhood, was out of control. If I was perfect, I would be okay.

I ask for a deeper and higher sense of presence, calm, and divine perfection of each situation, so that I may make unconditional love more important than anything.

In truth, I don't know how to do this. The most I can do is admit that my perfectionism is preventing me from living fully in joy.

I ask now to let go of how I think things should be, so I may elevate my consciousness and see the perfection in how things are. After all, there are so many things over which I have no control, so what is the point of fighting? Release me from my resistance to reality and allow me to find inner balance and inner perfection, and not expect to find it in the outer world.

May I experience more gratitude in the midst of turmoil and give myself the space to release my judgments of myself that tell me I am not enough, and turn my attention instead to the beauty to be found in life's imperfections.

I exhale and I experience the unbinding of the ties that have closed me in. Now I can let myself really breathe and be in my perfect, divine expression.

So be it!

19

The Importance of Feeling Unimportant

Some time ago, I was attending a women's conference, where I ran into a dear, young friend of mine. We were having coffee together during a break, and she said to me, "I feel very unimportant in these kinds of environments." I asked, "How so?" She said, "Well everyone is somebody. People have careers, books, credentials, and I feel like I am only at the starting point in my life. I feel like I'm nobody to these people." I chuckled and said, "You're definitely somebody to me because I care for you and think you are just the most wonderful girl."

But she still felt small and contracted. I said, "Imagine that we were all in a boat and the boat was sinking. We were all alerted to get into the life rafts filled with young people, older people, the crew, captain, and everybody else on board. How would you feel?"

"I would feel scared," she said. "Of course," I said. "But would you feel less important than the crew or the bestselling author behind you?"

"No, I would feel like we're all in it together," she replied.

That's exactly the point. Our ego and the hierarchy of the world makes us feel that there are important people and unimportant people. To some extent, this is true if you are looking at people through your worldly eyes, which assign value or worth to people according to their careers, celebrity status, material possessions, and so on. But this is a trap that can only cause unhappiness and restriction of our own expression.

My friend and I talked about how we all measure ourselves against other people who we perceive to have achieved more, to have done more, or to have more than us. It's even possible that there is a person out there who has decided that you're not as important as someone else because you don't have something that they have. You have to possess a lot of courage in order to feel good about whatever state you are in, and to know that you are in a constant process of growing, learning, and becoming. So don't place the additional burden of hierarchy on yourself. Our world is hierarchical, but our challenge as spiritual beings is to dismantle the hierarchy.

I once acted in a movie with Anthony Hopkins. I had a very small role as the housekeeper, but I felt so fortunate to get the part. Being with Hopkins and the renowned director James Ivory was a golden opportunity. When I arrived in London to play my scene with Hopkins, the lead actor, it was very easy to feel unimportant and "less than." It's normal to feel nervous and insecure, but hey, I had gotten the part. When I was talking to Hopkins, he must have sensed my anxiety. He turned to me and said in his wonderful and powerful way, "Yes, well, be Agapi! Be bold, and mighty forces will come to your aid." That was great advice. Whenever I feel insecure or apprehensive because of the people around me, I follow this advice. I summon my boldness and confidence, wherever I can find it, and know that there will always be other people who seem more successful, more in demand, richer, or more talented than I, but that doesn't make me less important than anyone else.

That's a distinction we all need to make. When you feel unimportant, tell yourself, "I give myself permission to be an important person in my life—because I am. I will take my space and my place in this world. I will claim my gifts and what I have and see what I want to create for myself." From that place of knowing your value, you can reach out and ask for help. Learn from people and connect with mentors, but always remember that your value does not depend upon your accomplishments.

This prayer is for when you hear the voice that tries to under-mine you and says you are not important, that other people are way more important than you. Make a habit of showing that voice the exit door.

The Prayer

Dear Beloved,

As I move into the world, I experience uncertainty about my importance, which keeps me from moving forward and asking for what I want—to connect with other people and to hear my own guidance and wisdom—and I'm feeling separate from others as I compare myself to what they've accomplished and what they have.

I ask to know my value and worthiness so I can see through the illusion that stops me from experiencing the fullness of me just as I am, accepting my life and myself in my own process. I ask that I may rise to my life with courage and confidence and look at this world as a stage on which everybody plays their part, and everybody's part is necessary to make the play complete.

Whatever tricks my ego has been playing, I ask that I outsmart that part of myself and become the master of it, that I take charge of the parts that make me feel I lack anything. Although I might not have what others have, it's a victory to know that the absence of those things does not make me less.

Right now, I rise up in myself. I expand my awareness to include a bigger vision of myself and my potential, and I ask that the spirit ignite that vision now, so I feel connected, aligned, and free.

I embrace this awareness and I ask that I may return to the place in me that knows my importance and claims it more often than not.

I let myself rejoice in my own spirit and aliveness as I move in a heart-driven way that knows no hierarchy or separation. I am grateful to play my part in this life and enjoy the immense variety of all the other players. I celebrate the richness of this life and its people.

So be it.

Quick God Fix for Feeling Unloved

Show me that you are here with me right now. I am willing to perceive new possibilities and feel connected and joyful in myself.

20

Our Divine Right to Heal

The other day, I was learning how to take out the seed of an avocado with a knife. You basically take the knife and bang it into the seed to pull it out, but I missed it and cut myself, and of course, I was bleeding quite a bit. I ran my finger under water, put it on ice, and covered it with a Band-Aid, but every time I took the Band-Aid off, it kept bleeding, and little traces of blood dripped onto the kitchen counter and floor. The next day, I dabbed on some peroxide and antibiotic cream, and the bleeding finally stopped.

This got me thinking about our wounds and how, when we are emotionally wounded, we put Band-Aids over our wounds in the form of external substitutes. We might focus too much on our physical appearance, throw ourselves into our work, or get lost in relationships because there is hurt within us that we don't want to look at. But when the Band-Aid comes off, the hurt is still there, showing us that there is still healing to be done.

Healing is uncovering the vulnerable parts in us that might be in pain or feel separated from others. When we are young, we learn to cover up those wounds because we feel we will fall apart if they are visible in a world that doesn't accept or nurture weakness. As we grow into our lives and start to make sense of our world, it takes tremendous compassion to truly see ourselves and acknowledge where the pain is: the times when we didn't get what we wanted or we got hurt. Pain can come from many different sources—our parents, our teachers, our peers, the circumstances we were born into. We all have a responsibility to look at our lives and acknowledge when we stopped expressing who we are, when we said no to ourselves, when we built boundaries and walls around our heart, our expressions, and our true selves.

So who is this wounded self? We don't carry wounds in our soul or spirit. The wounds are carried in the human part—the child in us, the adolescent, then the adult, and eventually the elderly person. These parts carry the hurt and disappointment. We can carry our hurts to the very end of our lives, but if we are willing to recognize the hurt, give it a voice, and not put a Band-Aid on it, we can heal and release it so that we can return to ourselves and our place of wholeness. With enough love and acceptance, you can heal. Maybe you can ask for that love and acceptance from a friend or family member, someone who can show you what unconditional love is. Or, if you choose to turn to a therapist, make sure they care for you and have a deeper understanding of the soul of who you are. You can always turn to your higher power and allow that unconditional love to guide you.

As I shared earlier, my wounded self had a lot to do with my parents' separation—I was powerless over the pain that my father caused my mother, and I didn't understand why they couldn't just love each other so we could be a happy family. Because I couldn't fix them, I made the decision that there was something wrong with me. This became the wounded part. So I became the giver, the lover, the person who brought warmth and kindness to alleviate any suffering I could; there was some good in how I transformed my wound. Later on, I experienced disappointment in love and that created loneliness and separation within myself. I wanted something "out there" that was not given to me, and I started to believe I couldn't experience intimacy, love, or connection with the opposite sex. So I began to learn how to be there for myself, love myself, accept myself, and give myself permission to be who I was, who I am, and who I am becoming.

A dear friend of mine, who is a very successful public speaker, shares this transformational story with his audiences about a time when he was a little boy in school. He raised his hand to tell his teacher he needed to go to the bathroom, so his teacher took him to the bathroom, stood over him, and said, "Go if you need to go." Obviously, he was so frightened in that moment that he could not pee. When he got back to the classroom, the teacher grabbed him by the collar and said to the whole class, "This boy is a liar. He said he had to go to the bathroom, but he was just pretending." Then she sent him to the corner and made him face the wall. This experience was extremely humiliating and intimidating for him, and he developed a stutter.

Through his inner work, he discovered that he was afraid speaking out would lead to punishment. It took him years of work to return to his true self and develop into a tremendous public speaker, sharing his message in front of many people. So often, an incident that happens in our lives gets locked in our unconscious, and we form beliefs about our lives and ourselves based on that pain. The hurt becomes cemented. Then, when we go after something we want to achieve or have in our lives, we run up against the wall of that belief. My friend's belief was that he would be punished if he spoke, and this belief was so powerful that he developed a stutter that took years to undo.

Just as a cut finger needs time and ointment in order to heal, the wounded parts of ourselves need expression and forgiveness and love to start the healing process. The healing cannot happen mentally, but it can happen from your soul level because that's where the love is. If you open up your doors, you allow the love to come in and help you experience the hurt. As you experience the hurt, know that on the other side there is peace, alignment, and joy. There is awe, gratitude, and, yes, even blissfulness because now you are no longer identifying with the wound but becoming grounded in the heart of who you are. So join me in this prayer in which we bring the wounded parts of ourselves into the light. You can fill in the gaps and sentences to start your own healing process and restore you to yourself.

The Prayer

Dear Beloved,

I know that there are parts of me that have experienced hurt: the hurt of how I wanted things to be that never were, the hurt that formed the wound that became so deep and left me with questions about why there was so much pain.

Now, I bring those parts into the light. I no longer need them, but I also do not know how to give them up because without them, who am I? Without them, I wonder if I will be left alone and feel even more alone on this earth.

I summon the courage to look at the wounded parts of me and invite your grace to begin healing them with love.

I claim that this experience no longer has a hold on me, and through forgiveness I can find the release to be freed and to be healed.

I ask that as I fall asleep tonight, like a magician, I will visit myself and transform this wounded self into strength, peace, and wholeness.

Show me the way. Allow me the great dignity and power of the spirit that works with me and in me to show me all that is possible.

So be it.

21

To Thine Own Self Be True

Betrayal comes in many forms. It's not always as obvious as discovering that your significant other has been cheating on you. Betrayal can occur when you hear of people speaking about you behind your back. It can occur when a friend withholds information from you, or you find that people you trusted cut you out of a deal at work. It can occur when people lie to you about something minor, but you can still feel a sense of betrayal. We can also feel betrayed by life when our expectations are not met.

One of the worst forms of betrayal occurs when we sabotage ourselves. We say we're going to do one thing and do another, or we violate our truth and values. For example, you might go on a first date and tell yourself you are going to wait to have sex. But the connection of the moment sweeps you away, and you forget the promise you made to yourself. You betray yourself by ignoring your inner guidance. In my own life, I've been too trusting of others, often ignoring the red flags because I didn't want to see who they really were. I didn't take care of myself or honor myself by listening to my better judgment.

When I first moved to New York from London, I got the lead role in the Greek production of *Lysistrata*. This was a big win for me because I was just starting out as an actor. The director let the cast know that he was still looking for a few additional actors for the chorus. At the time, I was attending an acting class, so I shared the information with my fellow students. One of the actors in the class went in for an audition, and the director thought she would be great for the lead. Since he had already cast me in the lead, he decided to split the role between us, which came as a shock to me.

It was a difficult situation to accept, but I tried to go along with it. In rehearsals, the director started to compare us to each other. He would point to the other actor as the example I should try to emulate. I started to lose my confidence; I felt completely deflated. I finally told the director that I no longer wanted to be part of the show. This was one of the most painful experiences of my life. I had betrayed myself by not taking care of myself and not protecting myself. I didn't have to be such a do-gooder and tell the class that the director wanted extras. When he proposed splitting the part, I could have put my foot down. Once we started rehearsing and he was comparing us, I could have spoken up and told him to stop. I might have channeled my anger and frustration into the role rather than feeling like a victim. But the truth is, some part of me lacked the confidence that I could carry the role on my own.

When I look back at the unconscious motivation that made me sabotage myself, I realize I had an underlying belief that I did not deserve my own success. I had to face the negative energy of my own self-doubt. It took me a long time to validate myself by trusting my intuition and my inner wisdom. Through reflection and prayer, I have strengthened my inner connection so I know when to be protective of my energy, my relationships, and, most of all, myself. Finding that still place beyond the chatter of the mind, the disturbances of the ego, and the rights and wrongs has allowed me to clear the path to knowing my truth and having the courage to stand by it.

That moment in my twenties was my first true understanding of what it would mean to be loyal to myself, when I started to build a solid relationship with myself. I had to learn not to betray my own judgment by believing other people's opinions or comparing myself to others. This was a pivotal moment in my life, when I embraced God as my partner and knew that I was not alone. Things started to shift for me once I became more in tune to the signs God was showing me. It's inevitable that we will act against ourselves, but these hard lessons often become the signposts on the path to our true selves. We learn to listen to our intuition and become better connected with our inner being. Prayer is an extraordinary way to renew our awareness of what it means to be loyal to our true selves.

The Prayer

Dear Beloved,

I bring forward the disturbance of my hurt feelings and the separation I am experiencing between myself and others.

I ask now for clarity and humility as I release my judgment of the situation so that I may see what is happening with love and light.

I ask that the higher wisdom in me prevail so that I may know how to stand by myself without defense or compromise but with the flexibility of my spirit that is mightier than the rigidity of this world.

I ask that I open the channels of communication with the different parts of myself as well as with any others who are in a similar situation.

*I ask that I not judge myself or others as right or wrong
but see the higher field of oneness and know that if I can
bring forward a higher consciousness, I will find resolution,
peace, and love, and transcend the pain of separation.*

*I forgive myself for forgetting that I am a beautiful being
and a beautiful person, and I offer compassion to myself for
my human experience.*

*I ask that I may bring closure to this experience of feeling
betrayed by myself so that I may restore myself and from
this moment on walk in the joy of being true to who I am.*

So be it.

Quick God Fix to Hear the Voice of Your Wisdom

ME: God, what do you have to say to me?

GOD: Shut up and let me love you.

ME: Thank you.

22

You Are Never Really Abandoned

Have you ever felt uncomfortable when you're alone? Have you experienced inner restlessness when you weren't surrounded by people? Do you feel a sense of being left out and abandoned? You might be dealing with unresolved abandonment issues.

As children, most of us look to our parents for support and safety. If at some point that is threatened, perhaps because the parents are having a conflict or are dealing with the stresses of their lives, we absorb that insecurity, feeling left alone to fend for ourselves. My sense of abandonment came when my parents separated, and my mother took my sister and me and raised us on her own. By the time I was two years old, my father started to leave my mother, living his own life and having extramarital affairs. My mother was devastated, alone, and unsupported. She had no career of her own, so she was totally dependent on him financially and emotionally. There she was, in a little home in Athens, Greece, with two children, raising us with a man who was increasingly irresponsible and distant. By the time my parents separated, I felt unsafe and unable to express my true feelings. It was like the stool I was sitting on suddenly had three legs instead of four and was wobbling. My family structure had completely shifted, and I had no ability to put the pieces back together. It took me years to address the feelings of anxiety and insecurity on my own, and to heal the parts of me that felt helpless.

At a very young age, we take on our parents' emotions. It's because we have no protective field around us to help distinguish what is ours and what is theirs. We feel everything. The brain starts to ask questions: Am I safe? Am I loved? Do I matter? Having an empathetic nature, I started to embody my mother's feelings of abandonment. Although my father adored me and my mother loved me deeply, I could not understand why I always had this feeling of displacement and disconnection. I never felt at home. For me, this manifested in my relationships with men, money, and work. I found safety in people who needed me and relied on me. Since I was young, I always attracted friends who had problems and needed me for support.

Unconsciously, I was attracting people I could give my friendship, comfort, and support to because I felt these people would never leave me. As wonderful as it is to give, it can also be a self-defense mechanism. My incredible love of being with people developed partly because the company of others buffered my feelings of abandonment.

Through my inner work and a lot of prayer, I realized how that feeling was first embodied in me. I chipped away at the different parts of it and I came to understand it; but it was not until I was writing this book that the bigger picture of my unconscious was revealed to me. As I prayed and asked for my higher power to show me what that feeling of abandonment was, the spirit in me showed up, and through grace, that emotional disturbance I lived with was released.

That is the power of grace that comes through prayer. I felt entirely different. Grace is like you're climbing a mountain, sweating and working, and then suddenly a balloon comes and lifts you up effortlessly to the top of the mountain. You see, we all have to do the inner work—the digging into our consciousness—to liberate ourselves. That is grace. All my life I felt responsible for my mother's feelings because I loved her. There is a sense of maturity that comes with the ability to distinguish which feelings are yours and which feelings belong to others. I can love someone and shine light on them, but my greatest gift is to feel intact and aligned with myself. You can pray for that shift in consciousness. So in this prayer, I ask you to examine your feeling of abandonment and how you can return to feeling safe within yourself. What triggers abandonment for you? Let us pray.

The Prayer

Dear Beloved,

I have a persistent feeling of abandonment locked within me. It shows up in my relationships, my work, and in many situations in my life. When I am by myself, I experience a longing to feel connection, to feel support, to feel that I am not alone in this world.

As much as I know the love that is around me and my family, and the love of spirit in me, there is a gap between what I feel and what is real. There is a missing link that I ask to be healed right now.

I ask that I may experience my own fullness and feel whole within myself.

I ask for grace to show me when I first experienced abandonment, where I lost the joy of being with myself, where I lost the deeper connection, where I lost my inner knowing that I am whole and complete. When was that promise broken?

May I find the courage to release this memory of feeling unsafe that lurks in my consciousness.

And so I open my heart now to that child in me that first embodied that memory, and I, like a loving parent, bring my heart, love, and wisdom to that child in me. Let the whisper of my spirit resonate in my ears, my heart, and my being, reminding me that I am safe, whole, and complete right now.

I replace the insecurity with feelings of trust, calmness, and quiet, and a solid foundation on which I can walk on this earth, feeling ever so grounded within myself.

I allow this moment to be sacred, and I know that I am not just okay; I am more than okay. I know that I can never be abandoned because I am always connected to the spirit.

I let go and I receive. I stand in silent reverence, and I evoke my joy.

So be it!

23

Stand in Your Mighty Self and Banish Self-Doubt

When I speak to a group of people, I often ask the group if there is anyone who experiences self-doubt. A lot of people raise their hands. I choose one person and invite them onto the stage. I ask them, "Is it okay if I touch you?" Usually, they say yes, and I take them by the shoulders, shake them, and say, "Shake it off shake it off shake it off!" They usually start to laugh and so does the group. I say, "Good! It's working." There is nothing like changing your physiology to shift your psychology.

If you're feeling self-doubt, you have to respond physically rather than mentally. When I was working toward my masters in psychology, I created "The Agapi Method." Here's how it works: A client comes to see a therapist and is ready to start talking. The therapist puts music on—my music of course is from *Zorba the Greek*—and has the client dance their heart out. When they're out of breath, the therapist says, "Now go ahead and tell me what's on your mind." It's incredible how movement dissipates the energy stuck in the brain. When we release dopamine, the feel-good hormone, we feel good!

Self-doubt is insidious. Instead of being an angel on your shoulder, it's a devil whispering undermining thoughts that cause you to let your doubt take the lead, and you become immobilized, unable to move forward, and create what you want in your life. It's very important that we understand the part of us that is like Darth Vader, sabotaging our ability to feel bold and daring and our willingness to take risks. It is to our advantage to recognize it and name it and not identify with it. Self-doubt is a conditioned negative pattern that undermines us, but we can take authority over it by knowing that we are bigger than it and can rise above it. As much as it's trying to undermine us, we can undermine it. It takes courage to stand up to the parts of ourselves that are doubtful, negative, depressed, and hostile—and to know that there is always a way beyond our self-doubt by expanding our consciousness and connecting with the higher wisdom in us. That's where I have learned to exercise my prayer muscle. In the moment, when I feel self-doubt creep up on me,

I turn my focus inward and call upon my higher power to lift me up.

There have been many situations in my life in which I had to overcome the feeling of defeat in order to achieve the results I wanted. When I was raising money for a project called "Conversations with the Goddesses," my one-woman show that I co-produced with PBS, I went to the Greek community to raise money. I reached out to every Greek I ever knew, and a lot of them would say to me, "What a wonderful and ambitious project! Good for you that you want to do this." But no one was writing a check. I finally hit a wall, but I remember looking at this piece of paper that my spiritual teacher had given to me that said, "Continue on at all costs." I knew I was eventually going to raise the money, and every no I heard was getting me closer to a yes, so I decided to turn it into a game. I went for a walk and talked to myself, summoning up the strength to look at every no as an opportunity to not give up and not cave in but to keep going. I decided to call one of my Greek friends who was extremely wealthy. With all my goddess power, I said to him with gusto, "Listen, Dennis, send me something, anything!" My Greek chutzpah and charm got to him because I wasn't coming from a place of lack or fear but from an excitement about and a belief in my project. He said, "Okay, I'm sending you $5,000." The next morning, the FedEx envelope arrived. I opened it and indeed there was the check. I jumped up and down yelling, "Yes, yes, yes!" because I knew that the gate was now open for me to receive more. I had to break through my resistance to asking and receiving; this was an extraordinary victory, of not letting the doubt win. Next, I called Dennis's best friend, another wealthy Greek man, and I said to him, "John, Dennis gave me $5,000. Will you match it?" And indeed he said, "Okay, I will send you another $5,000." The tsunami of fundraising was underway, and I was thrilled to witness it. I found more people, Greek and not Greek, who kept donating until we raised what was needed to produce the special.

This was a very powerful experience that lifted me whenever I doubted myself or wanted to give up. I had to transform defeat and not let the doubt inside of me win. These aspects of ourselves zap our energy and deplete us, and we must outsmart and outlast them. If we stop and become still, we will discover that there is a centered place inside of us that is connected to our spirit, soul, and source. The negative voices in our head put a veil in front of our light, wholeness, and power. If we have the courage to step back and ask for help—and this is where prayer comes in—we will find that the blocks and limitations can be lifted so we can see the possibilities and opportunities that lie ahead of us. If we turn against ourselves and give in to self-doubt, we are going to feel defeated. It is up to each one of us to return to the power of our inner connection and use our mental dominion to take authority over the parts in us that hesitate.

This prayer is a call to your strength, resilience, and resourcefulness, so it's really a prayer to call forward the spiritual warrior in you who is unafraid. At some point in our lives we all do battle with those parts of ourselves, and we owe it to ourselves to turn toward the light of our true selves.

The Prayer

Dear Beloved,

I quiet myself and come into the presence of my heart.

I call forward right now the power of my spirit that lives in me, that sustains and gives me life. Like a positive tsunami of strength, will, persistence, and resilience, I let it move through my body, mind, and emotions and steady me; and as I'm steady in myself, I feel enveloped in a feeling of trust, and I see myself standing on the solid ground beneath my feet. I give myself permission to move forward to my next action with spirit on my side.

As I witness the part of me that wants to cave in, give up, and give in to doubt and fear, I know that there is a mighty force in me that is connected to the infinite.

I close my eyes, and I allow myself to be bathed in this mighty presence of the peaceful warrior that shows me how to carve my life's path.

I march, I run, I hop, I summersault. I use my body to move through this wall that is trying to shut me out, block my awareness, undermine me, and make me feel less than who I am.

I find the still point in me and settle there, letting the part of me that knows me come alive. I resonate with the fullness of myself. I am deeply grateful for being heard and feeling seen.

So be it!

IV

Overcoming

24

How to Get Out of a Toxic Environment

I was conducting a workshop in which people were focusing on what they wanted to change in their lives. One of the participants was a woman who shared that she felt tremendous hostility—a dark, toxic energy—from one of her colleagues at work, every time they interacted. My first question to her was: why was she choosing to stay in this job? Her answer was that she was grateful to have a job with good pay and benefits, and she was scared to leave in case she couldn't find another job that was right for her. She believed this was the only job in the world that she could get.

I have encountered a lot of people who have found themselves in difficult situations at work that leave them feeling drained and worn out, but they are fearful to leave, so they live in anxious dread of going to work every day. They are afraid that leaving their job means they won't be able to provide for themselves or their families, and they don't trust that there will be another job for them. Those are legitimate fears. At the same time, if you are in a state of fear and paralysis, you will be unable to see new opportunities or solutions to your situation.

If you have a problem at work, it's very important that you bring the spirit and consciousness of your God-self to help you transform this challenging situation. Once you acknowledge the part of you that feels trapped, imprisoned, and suffocated in a job, you'll realize your life and your days are too precious to spend in a miserable situation.

Of course, there are times in life when we must endure jobs that we don't like in order to make a living. A wonderful friend of mine, who is a talented actor and has had a series of great roles on Broadway, was not able to work during the coronavirus pandemic. He had no choice but to go back to waiting tables during the in-between period. When I asked him how it was going, he told me that he didn't like it and it was difficult to work in a mask and at a distance, but he was grateful to make the extra money in order to pay his rent. His focus on gratitude made the difficult aspects of his job more bearable.

We can always empower ourselves with choices; sometimes,

the most powerful choice we can make is to shift our attitude. Shifting our attitude toward gratitude can transform even the most difficult conditions. At other times, we can enlist our courage to get ourselves out of those situations that rob us of enthusiasm for our work. No matter what your job is, if you lack a sense that you are contributing, do yourself the favor of opening your mind and heart to other possibilities.

Find friends and allies who want the best for you and can support you in tapping into your strength, trust, and confidence in yourself. This is where I feel prayer can be helpful. In prayer you start to remember who you are and know that you deserve uplifting and energizing work. It's worthwhile to find an occupation in which you feel valued and fulfilled, and through which you can contribute and grow.

The Prayer

Dear Beloved,

Here I am, in an unfulfilling and challenging work situation, in which I feel I am being robbed of joy, enthusiasm, and meaningful collaboration.

I ask for the support and guidance to find a new pathway.

I sit in my stillness and find my quiet place. I open my heart and acknowledge my sadness at missing the connectivity of creative work. I release these feelings here, in the safety of your presence.

I let go of the ways I judge myself for not creating a work environment in which I can feel the human spirit and the joy of doing good work.

I ask that I may renew my trust and listen to my inner wisdom so that I can follow the leads to something new. I rise up within myself to know there are other ways to work and there is so much possibility for my life.

I cast my fear aside and open my vision to see what action I must take to find work that I love among people who value my contribution.

I restore my faith in the abundant universe that I belong to. I belong to the whole; I belong to life.

I trust the miracle of life, and I will keep trusting until the miracle arrives.

Most of all, I love myself through it, and I will not withdraw my love from myself, which is the greatest miracle of all.

So be it.

You're Bigger Than Your Fear

My parents fought in the Second World War. When the Nazis invaded Greece, my father was captured and taken to a concentration camp for a year and a half. My mother fought back with the Greek Resistance in the Red Cross, caring for patients and hiding Jews in cabins in the mountains. At one point, she came face-to-face with the Nazis who marched into the cabin she was stationed in. As they started to shoot, she stood up, and with a mighty inner force said to them in perfect German, "Put down the guns. You have no right to shoot. We are with the Red Cross." She often described what an extraordinary moment this was: seeing the Nazis obey her and lower their three machine guns. She also had the audacity to tell one of the Nazis who had picked up her comb, "Can I have my comb back? Because I need it more than you!" She often told me and my sister, "I have faced fear dead on, and I overcame it, so nothing scares me anymore in my life." She paved the path to fearlessness for us and so many others who knew her.

Though she passed away many years ago, we feel her palpable presence all the time. When I ask her spirit what she would do in times like these, she says, "Don't be consumed by the news, put your full attention in anything you do, eat slowly, live fully every moment, and darling, don't give into fear. You're bigger than that."

My mother's trust in life always propelled her to take action and claim mental dominion over the uncertain circumstances of her life. When we were in Greece as teenagers, my sister wanted to study at Cambridge. We lived in a one-bedroom apartment in Athens, and the idea of going to England seemed out of reach, but my mother told my sister, "Let's go to Cambridge and look at the university to see what it is like to live and study there." She brought this experience to life for my sister so that her dream could become a reality. The power of walking through the town of Cambridge and imagining herself studying on campus formed pictures of attending university there in my sister's mind. This was absolutely masterful of my mother.

When they returned from their visit, my sister devoted many hours to working hard and studying for the entrance exam, and indeed, two years later, she was admitted to Cambridge.

My dream was to study acting at the Royal Academy of Dramatic Arts (RADA). Finding my way to the audition required asking many different people for help. One of my mother's gifts was her fearlessness in doing just that. She demonstrated a certain chutzpah when it came to seeking out support; she asked with such graciousness and bravery that people wanted to help her. She asked around, trying to find someone who had gone to RADA, and she found an actor in Athens who had graduated from the academy. She contacted him, and he recommended a teacher in London who could prepare me for my audition.

When we moved to London, I met and began studying with this acting teacher, but it was not a great experience. She couldn't really draw out my talent, and she discouraged me from even trying to become an actor. When I went home and told my mother, completely devastated that this teacher didn't believe in me, my mother didn't miss a beat. She told me that this wasn't the right teacher for me because she didn't get me. Not only that, but my mother also had the audacity to ask that teacher if she would recommend a different teacher who could work with me. Talk about fearlessness! We found a wonderful director from the Royal Academy who took me on, saw the talent in me, and was able to foster it. She gave me the confidence to audition for the academy, and indeed, I got in.

I was very blessed to have a mother who didn't collapse in the midst of making things happen. She saw life as her own school of possibilities and she entered that arena with gusto. When I look at people who are truly fearless, who have no script for how to make things happen but still get what they want, I see a spirit that transcends the human condition and says, "I will keep going at all costs!" Often, the possibilities will keep showing up, and if they do not, these people keep going.

If you are experiencing fear in your life, evoke the spirit of the extraordinary people in the world who have broken barriers and overcome hardships, and access that place from which you can see and act beyond the fear. As you move forward in your life, what stops you? What are you afraid of? Name it, whatever it is, and take authority over it. Be inspired by the fearless spirit, which has been demonstrated by the great leaders of our world and also lives in you. Evoke my mother's spirit and that of so many others who have overcome so much to be where they are. Find your role models as you seek to transform your own circumstances and discover the courage to expand beyond your fear and create the life you want.

The Prayer

Dear Beloved,

As I move forward in my journey, I ask to find the courage to move past my fear, knowing that the mighty spirit that lives in me is so much bigger than my fear.

Show me how to transform my fear into trust and my insecurity into confidence. Show me how to transform my scared voice into my sacred voice.

Let me walk this path, step by step, holding your invisible hand, hearing the inner guidance in me. Although I might not feel it fully or comprehend it, I am willing to let my higher power take the lead.

Show me where the opportunities are and lead me to the support I need, so I can see my vision clearly and draw strength from it.

I understand that the fear I am experiencing is produced by the primitive part of my brain that is driven to survive. When I turn to prayer and meditation, I become quiet and still, and in that space I feel the presence of love, compassion, and joy because I remember that I don't have to give in to my fear. As I say these words, I feel a release of what binds me and keeps me from moving ahead. I feel a wave of happiness in knowing that I don't have to live in wishful thinking, that I can live in action. I move from I can't to I am.

So, as I move forward in taking the next steps, I see the sword of strength that clears my pathway so I can move with determination, trust, and positive energy, which are always available to me.

As I speak these words, I release the illusion that I am walking alone, and I receive the support that shows me in practical, small ways that I can expand beyond my fear.

So be it.

Prayer for Feeling like an Outsider

Dear Beloved,

When I am at work, attending a social event, or spending time with my friends and family, I feel that I am on the outside looking in. I ask for a way to break through that wall and see the illusionary field I have built around me for what it is. It has become part of my life and separates me from others and from my heart. It makes up stories that I don't belong and everyone else has been given the keys to life and I missed out.

I ask that this veil and this belief be lifted from me now. I am willing. I dare to ask and I dare to know that it is possible to pierce through this imprisonment that I have put myself in so that I can experience the fulfillment of myself and learn to love myself exactly where I am.

I ask for the love that is in me to shine through and for the light to come in and help me see through new eyes of inclusiveness. In this asking, I receive.

So be it.

26

The Discouragement Trap

Discouragement is the enemy of the human spirit. There should be a big flashing sign that pops up, Beware of Discouragement! as we travel on our life journeys. It's important to stay ahead of it and outsmart it. I know discouragement intimately, and it has visited me on many occasions.

Imagine going after something you want—a mate, a creative goal, a new job, or better health—and you encounter setbacks, challenges, and rejections. Perhaps you decide to start dating, and on the fifth or sixth date, the feeling that this relationship is not going to work out creeps up on you. The voice of discouragement starts to whisper, "This is not going to work out; it's never going to work out. I'm feeling deflated; I lack the confidence to keep going." You feel a wave of doubt closing in on you, causing you to shut off your heart, your creativity, and your fun. You feel like you are walled in and you want to give up. I've had many setbacks with my creative expression. I would start on a project like writing a book and not feel the creative flow or the inspiration. Instead of accepting that as a natural part of the creative process, I would get discouraged and down on myself, and it would become challenging to keep going.

At that moment of defeat, the challenge is to not identify with that feeling of discouragement but instead to observe it from a distance. You can have mastery over yourself and, in fact, it's in that very moment when circumstances are not going your way that you can empower yourself by calling forward your God presence, which is far more powerful than negative emotions.

The emperor of Rome, Marcus Aurelius, withstood the plague in his empire for fourteen years and, in a collection of his notes, *Meditations,* he shared the wisdom of his journey. He talks about examining everything you encounter in your life and using it for your growth and to your advantage. He writes, "If you are troubled by external circumstances, it is not the circumstances that trouble you but your own perception of them and that is in your power to change at any time." He tells us, "This too comes from God and no matter what, I will treat everything remembering that it has no power to weaken me, to pay me harm unless I let it." When you start to feel the pull of discouragement, remember that this power of perception is available to you if you choose it. This choice in each moment is where our freedom lies.

Give your discouragement a visual. Mine is a fire-breathing dragon with fangs and talons that is trying to extinguish me. If you give it a name and an image, you can start to have some fun with it. Yours might not be as dramatic. Maybe it's a short and slimy little goblin who comes to tell you how lonely you are, or that other people have what you want, that you are not loved or valued, that you will never amount to anything. When that goblin shows up, it makes you want to crawl into a hole and hide. But your discouragement only has power if you feed it. When you keep it outside of yourself, it might still try to talk to you, but you don't have to listen to what it says.

Anytime you encounter the conniving, devious, manipulative, and uninvited energy of discouragement, you can bring this prayer to your heart, with any words you want to add, to override this energy and know that the power invested in you from the spirit is far more real, powerful, and loving.

The Prayer

Dear Beloved,

I come present in my heart, quiet myself, attune myself to my breath, and turn my focus inward. I take a long, slow, deep breath, and I exhale my anxiety, my worry, and my tension. I take another long, slow, deep breath, and I exhale, too, the feelings of defeat that have taken over me. As I breathe in, I allow myself to relax, move into profound calm and peace, and create space inside of my body, my emotions, and my mind to bring a sense of trust and a new vision for what I'm working through.

Although the discouraged part of me wants to give up and can't see a way through this, I affirm that there is a way out of this contraction I've been feeling around my life in the areas of expression, love, and connection, and the lack of enthusiasm that I have for moving on and creating new opportunities for myself.

I'm open to receive inspiration and joy, to see new horizons where I am not seeing any, to see how this invisible light that works within me can delight me. I let it transform these thoughts that have invaded my being and tried to rob me of the newness of possibilities, creativity, and actions, because they put doubt in my heart and mind.

Right now, I breathe in that holy spirit, the comforter, and I begin to feel the joy of my thoughts that whisper to me how valued, loved, and connected I am. I allow myself to receive this spirit and rekindle the spark in me to keep going, to be the captain of my own ship, initiating new actions, propelled forward with the wind in my sails anchored in my emotional strength.

I now start to feel the tenderness of my spirit encouraging me to keep going, not forcing results or outcomes. Through this offering of my desires, I allow the transformation to unfold in a natural state of being.

So now, in my silence, I receive in my beingness, and as I am shown the possibilities of my life I experience the blessings of every moment.

I thank you. I am grateful.

So be it.

27

Finding the Wisdom in Your Disappointment

I have had my fair share of disappointments. There was a big event in Santa Barbara at which my sister was being honored, and I had invited a man as my date. The event was at 7:00 p.m., and at about 4:30 p.m., as I was starting to get ready, I got a call from the man saying that he was stuck in terrible traffic from Los Angeles and would not be able to make it. I felt incredibly disappointed, with a knot in my stomach. I had counted on him to show up and escort me to this very important event. I wanted to be with someone, and I was now stranded. I called a dear friend of mine who came to the rescue and escorted me to the event.

A few days later, I told my spiritual teacher about the

incident, and he said to me, "You have disappointment running in you as a theme, and you have to change that track so that things can start working out. You have to find the beginning of the thread." I had never really looked at it that way. I was just used to disappointment in my life, but indeed, it was a theme that started at a very young age. I was disappointed to witness the discord between my parents in their marriage. They couldn't be happy together, and my father's unfaithfulness hurt my mother so deeply. I felt helpless to do anything about it. I was disappointed by romantic relationships in which I was attracted to men who didn't feel the same way about me, and by friendships in which people broke their word or didn't show up for me the same way that I would show up for them. I felt like I was constantly being let down. I was also extremely disappointed by my acting career. I never got the roles that I wanted, and projects that I put a lot of energy and effort into never materialized.

When we are disappointed or feel let down, we think that something is wrong with us—that we're failing ourselves, that life is against us, that we'll never get what we want—and we collapse. Instead of moving forward with the power that we have to attract the opportunities that are right for us, we give up. I have met many people who cannot move past disappointment. It's hardest when they are disappointed in themselves.

I had told myself that the man I invited to the event was wonderful, and I had built up this fantasy that we would develop a relationship. It's true that we had a good time together and were attracted to each other. He was intelligent and charming. And so am I! But I didn't know who this man really was. So when he didn't show up, the disappointment was crushing. When we have a distorted view of something we hope for but don't know enough about, we set ourselves up for disappointment. When it doesn't happen, we feel betrayed, and we tell ourselves stories about why it didn't happen—about ourselves, about life—and we make all sorts of false assumptions.

What do you say to yourself in that moment when things don't work out? When the guy didn't show up for the date, I told myself it was because I wasn't desirable enough. When I wasn't getting the roles I wanted, I told myself I didn't have what it took to be a successful actor. These limiting beliefs interfere with your sense of self, and as a result, you start to doubt yourself and shut off your heart. You withdraw from life. When my mother saw me sinking into disappointment, she would often say, "Darling, change the channel. You've been going down the road to disappointment for two days now and that's enough." My suggestion is to give yourself a time limit of forty-eight hours to be upset, mad, or resentful, and then return to your ability to reset, learn from your disappointment, and bless the experience because it has made you more aware of what *is* for you and what *is not* for you.

I have found that the best key for letting go of disappointment is the courage to look it straight in the face and take ownership and responsibility. Ask yourself: What did I not want to see? What was I blinded to? What is the lesson and the awareness for me here? In my experience with my flaky date, I learned that I am too quick to project what I want to see onto other people. It's a certain lack of discernment and wisdom. Instead of stepping back and seeing people and situations as they are, I tend to live in wishful thinking—I wish this man to be so, so therefore I will project the qualities onto him that would make him so. I will project the prince onto the frog, but the frog is still the frog, and it is me who is disappointed. But, if we look at our disappointments from a higher perspective, they become opportunities to learn how to make choices that can work for us.

It takes inner awareness and digging in to find out what disappointment is really teaching you. Be mindful of the decisions and choices you make and be willing to forgive yourself when they don't work out. Don't be hard on yourself. Disappointment is part of the human experience. This prayer is for anyone stuck in disappointment to see a way out.

The Prayer

Dear Beloved,

I ask for the inner light to shine on me and my disappointment right now. I quiet myself and bring myself to stillness.

I ask that I may let go of blaming myself so that I may realize that I had simply placed my energy, focus, and attention onto something that was not meant for me. I ask that I may release the pain and the hurt, the feeling that I am lacking in something, and the feeling that my dream has collapsed.

I find myself in this empty field, where once there was a garden; now it is barren. I ask that you may make this ground fertile again, a ground in which new seeds can be planted and sprout—seeds of trust, seeds of renewed energy and enthusiasm, and seeds of strength to nurture the new possibilities that are there for me.

I ask that I may not judge my future based on what happened in the past, and that I may not hold myself hostage to this disappointment. As hard as it is now to see a new way, I ask that you show me the light shining for me on the possibilities for my life. Give me the patience to discover new ways of being, renew my faith in relationships, and trust my creativity. Let me see this one situation in its own unique way and not let the disappointment seep through the bigger vision of my life. This is just one scene in my movie; help me to know there are many other wonderful scenes to come.

I ask that I may know the power of letting go, moving on, and turning my attention to the bigger picture of my life.

I ask that I may keep a smile in my heart and soften the harsh edges of my demands on myself and my life so that I may have a kinder and more compassionate understanding of my human journey and embrace the lightness of my being.

I'm grateful. I give this over to the light within, and I go free.

So be it.

Quick God Fix for When You Receive Bad News

I step back and take a moment to find my peace. I call on the presence to alleviate the pain of this bad news I just received. I ask for the guidance of my higher wisdom, and the light to move within me and transform me to my stillness and peace and keep my heart open.

28

Reframing Failure to Your Advantage

We've all had the experience of embarking on a new project with trepidation, wondering, "How is it going to unfold?" There was a time in my life when I wanted to produce a PBS special based on my book *Conversations with the Goddesses.* My book had come out and was very well received. I had been doing my one-woman show at different museums, colleges, and theaters, and it was a fulfilling experience for me, as I was sharing my love, knowledge, and wisdom of the Greek goddesses.

I wanted to do this special for PBS. I had no idea how to go about it—I had never produced before—so I started by going backward. I opened my organizing book and wrote, "Conversations with the Goddesses Special: Done," and I put a check mark next to it. I think that's a great way to start a project or something you've never done before. I strategically broke down all the steps I would need to take to move forward: meet with PBS executives, find a producer, raise the money, write a script, find a location, and select a tentative date. I wrote the necessary steps in my book so I could look at them every day.

By that time in my life, I was thoroughly grounded in my belief and experience that God is my partner, and so I affirmed along the way that I was doing this in partnership with the spirit. Indeed, I started to take the next steps—I called a friend who introduced me to PBS, and PBS sent a producer to me. This producer was perfect and absolutely loved the project. Every email he sent me was titled "Moving forward with the goddesses." Indeed, that's what we did. We raised money for the special; I reached out to every Greek I knew—I must have heard ten noes before my first yes—but I knew that I was going to produce this project.

We found the perfect location in the garden of my spiritual center. People volunteered to help me, I wrote the script, and most of all I experienced a bubbling joy knowing that I was creating this piece of work that I was so passionate about. A wonderful set designer was introduced to me and decided to do the set on a very small budget. I memorized everything because it was being recorded live. It was remarkable! The pieces were coming together one by one, and I trusted that, no matter the obstacles, I was going to make this happen.

The last step was deciding what to wear. I wanted it to be modern while still evoking the spirit of the goddesses. I knew I did not want to be in a Greek goddess toga; I wanted something ethereal and magical. I must have gone to every single department store. I searched and searched, and when I found nothing, it occurred to me to ask for help from my inner goddess, Aphrodite. Soon after, I was guided to a shop in Beverly Hills that had the perfect chiffon gown for me, on sale, in the colors of Greek vases—terra-cotta and red. It was absolutely perfect! I was moved to tears when I put it on. I felt the spirit of the goddesses embodied in me when wearing this gorgeous outfit.

The day of the performance arrived. There we were, in an outdoor goddess garden setting. There were two hundred people present. Lights, cameras, and the California night sky—ready for action. It was one of the most magical days of my life. I felt I had stepped into a field of energy that was beyond this world, and as I performed the piece, I felt completely connected and enveloped by grace and spirit; it was flawless. Everyone who was there, including the director and producer, said it was an incredible, magical experience. Of course, we all thought this was going to be a smash hit. I'll never forget my producer saying this would be bigger than any show on PBS and that people were going to love it.

The show was edited and ready to go. But then, much to my dismay, they launched it as a pledge for PBS on a very small station in Newark at a terrible time, late at night. The show didn't do well during that broadcast, and the rest of PBS decided not to pick it up. We were all devastated.

Talk about disappointment. This was a big one. I had put so much into it—so much energy, time, and creativity. I had taken care of every detail, but I did not know much about producing, and making production decisions was not up to me. I felt that I had hit rock bottom, and I didn't know how I would climb out of it. I was so sad and dumbfounded. I asked God, "What went wrong? What happened? What didn't I see?" And of course, I judged myself as a failure.

Not long after, I was sitting at my desk bemoaning my fate when I received a random email: "Dear Agapi, last night I was watching PBS, and suffering in a tremendous amount of pain from endometriosis, when your show came on. I loved everything that you said, and I felt myself laughing, crying, and relating the goddesses to women in my life. Thank you a thousand times—your words gave me more relief in one hour than doctors have in two painful years!" I felt tears of joy pouring down my face, as though God was giving me my answer. One life had been touched by this work and who knows how many more?

As the days went on, more and more messages arrived, each person acknowledging how much they loved and valued the special. This was one of the greatest lessons of my life: so many times, things don't work out the way we plan or expect, but it's not because the world is against us, or because God wants us to be miserable or to punish us. Sometimes, things happen so we can gain understanding in our disappointment and learn that things are not always what they seem to be. These emails and letters validated the depth of the inner experience I had in producing the show. No one could take that away from me. The joy and fulfillment I had in completing it is mine and has enriched my life.

This experience reminded me that success is not necessarily an outer accomplishment but more of an inner experience. I've been able to apply that to many experiences in my life. Life is generous in allowing us to learn lessons from the things that we believe have not worked out. The awareness we gain about ourselves and our lives can be so enriching and invaluable that it is a success in itself. So, when you look at projects that you've started or are about to embark on, remember that the beauty of this creation is that you are not going to be given a manual, but you might be the one writing a manual for yourself and others.

Every turn in your life might not meet you with a glorious sunrise, but it will meet you with the elements that you need so that you can gain in wisdom, resilience, and vision. The crumbling of our expectations—as hurtful and despairing as it might feel—is the golden opportunity to return home to the fullness of ourselves. This prayer asks, when embarking on a new journey, for trust that you will always be guided, and if you arrive at an unexpected destination, there, too, spirit will meet you.

The Prayer

Dear Beloved,

I come present in my heart. I quiet myself, and I lift myself in the expansive realm of your loving presence and your effervescent joy of my spirit.

I bring into the light my feelings that I have failed in this project, relationship, job, or other endeavor on which I embarked with such hope and expectation. I bring into the light my feelings of disappointment that this did not turn out the way I wanted it to. I ask right now that I am able to release these feelings.

I have these questions in my heart: What happened? Where did this go wrong? What is the lesson for me to learn in this? *I hear the voice of my wisdom telling me to be patient as the lessons are revealed to me, and reminding me that I am not to blame. Let me see what I might do differently next time without judging myself this time. Allow me to have compassion for the human part of me that hurts because things did not go the way I hoped they would.*

Help me see that failure is not the opposite of success but rather a part of the journey to success. Let this experience not snuff out my magic and joy. Renew in me the energy and curiosity to try new things and take on challenges. Let me return to the beauty, soulfulness, and majesty of the spirit I sense and know in me and in the creative process.

I ask that the light illuminate this experience and bring peace to my heart and return me to the flow of possibility in my life.

So be it.

29

In the Eye of the Hurricane: Finding Calm in Crisis

When I speak to audiences, I ask them what they want most in their lives. Of course, things like money, love, free time, or health are mentioned, but the thing that people most want is inner peace. Many people interpret that as wanting their negative mind to leave them alone so that they can be calm. From a place of inner peace, everything else is worthwhile. You can create more of the things you want.

But how do we get to this inner peace we all long for? What is it that robs us of our peace?

One of my favorite images is the eye of a hurricane. The storm is swirling around, but in the middle, there is absolute stillness. We have to find that center in us—the eye of the hurricane—to anchor and root ourselves in that place of inner calm and expansion, even in the midst of the insecurity, the unknown, and the pain. It's not easy to do, but it's worth all the effort, practice, and focus we can devote to it, in order to find our center, which is connected to the eternal peace within us.

Many years ago, my sister visited me in New York and shared with me that she was going to get a divorce. I remember feeling this incredible heartache. The thought of the hardship two wonderful people and their kids had to go through saddened me to my core. It reminded me of my parents' separation, and I was so devastated by the news that I couldn't even call anyone to ask for support. So I decided to pray. I closed the curtains of my apartment, lit a candle, and asked with all my heart that the pain I was feeling be lifted from me. There was a presence that came over me and communicated a story to me. This presence brought me to a higher perspective. It was the year 3005, and my sister's divorce was long gone from this earth. No one in my family was known on earth any longer, and it was very different from the world I once knew. This presence communicated to me that we had all moved into the spirit, where we were gloriously united with the divine. When I came out of the experience, it was still 1998, but I felt lifted and at peace. It was one of the most profound experiences of prayer that I have had. I felt that everything was going to be okay, and of course, more than two decades later, that is so true.

When we go through incredibly painful and catastrophic events in our lives that take us into the deep unknown and shake everything inside of us, prayer can be a lifeline to a deeper perspective. When we can find perspective, we find our way out, we find solutions, and we find the comfort we need in that moment. So, let us pray and call forward this mighty force of our peace, knowing that this peace has a hidden force that can move mountains, bring healing to the sick, provide stillness in the eye of the storm, quiet the turbulent waters, and steady the earthquakes. Let's find it in us and bring it out into the open.

The Prayer

Dear Beloved,

We ask to move into a place of calmness, to move away from any disturbance, fear, separation, or judgment, and we ask that we let it go to a higher place where it shall be transmuted and dissolved into nothingness.

We ask for the light to embrace us on all levels of our

consciousness, from the top of our head to the soles of our feet.

We see ourselves filled and protected by this light that brings us wholeness, peace, and love.

This beautiful and warm energy is right now entering into the very bottom of our solar plexus, where the emotions and disturbances lie. We say, "Peace, be still," and know that we are whole.

We ask now that this peace move us into the next action in our lives—whatever little ordinary thing we have to do— and bring us the joy of being alive at this moment. We open our hearts and receive all the goodness, with gratitude for all the people we love and who are with us.

We ask that we may know that leading from our heart on every level is where the power of our peace lies. Whether we are awakening, interacting, working, cooking, cleaning, speaking on the phone, or walking on the street, we see ourselves leading from our hearts and leading forward with this enormous wave of peace.

We feel it, we breathe it, we embody it, and ever so gently we become one with this inner peace. No matter what disturbance comes from the outside, whether it is something we hear in the news, or something that didn't go well in our work life or with a loved one, we do not say "You interrupted my peace." Peace is all-inclusive; peace takes in every area of life and includes the dark, the bad, the lonely, and the suffering.

We do not resist what comes our way, and we don't resist how we feel every day, but we lean back and we let it pass through us. Like a sieve, we sift away what is not needed until the gold of peace remains. Do not say, "This is peace and this is not peace," because when you bridge the separation, peace is always present.

As you gaze from within, feel the light, and in the light, you will be lifted and become a conduit, a transformer, and a magical whisperer of love and peace.

Allow this peace to settle in your heart like a higher but calmer vibration that is as real as anything in your life. In the silence of this peace, listen for your inner messages, your inner prompts, and take in all your goodness and all the goodness that already exists on this earth.

So be it.

30

Having the Freedom to Choose How You React

I was playing a role in the musical *Never on Sunday* at a small venue in Hollywood with a lot of Greek-American actors, and I was so elated to have gotten a wonderful supporting role. But we had a director who was a complete bully—impossible to talk to or reason with. She treated the actors with absolutely no respect. All of us shared this view of her and talked about it on our breaks, but I wanted to keep my role in the production so I put up with it.

Every time I drove to rehearsal, I had a knot in my stomach and wanted to punch her, but I couldn't, so I put all that energy into my performance. One night, I was having dinner with my spiritual teacher and shared my struggle, asking for advice.

He took out a piece of paper and wrote, "Continue on at all costs," and he signed it and handed it to me. I still have that piece of paper in a frame on my desk. It changed my mindset, and I was able to continue with a greater spirit of cooperation, not feeling like a victim.

At the end of each performance, the director would ask us to break down the set and clean up the theater because classes were held there the next morning. Every night we had to break down the set, and every day we had to put the set back up—that's called love of your craft!

One night, I wanted to have drinks with my friends, but she asked me to clean the bathrooms before I left, and so I did, but as I did, I seethed with anger. I was so frustrated by her constant demands and her disregard for us. The next night, she asked me to clean the seats before I left and something different happened inside me. My heart was so full of the joy of performing and the incredible love from the audience that I started to clean the seats with absolutely no resistance. I suddenly saw this woman for who she was. I saw her with compassion, but more, I felt a deep compassion for myself.

My heart opened up so much that I started to cry. At that moment, as I let go of my resistance, I experienced the blessing of transformation. Ever since my spiritual teacher had given me the advice to continue on at all costs, I had begun to transform the parts of me that were judging her, believing that I was right and she was wrong. Every day I prayed for guidance to show me a way to surrender to the reality of this difficult situation; at the same time, I prayed for compassion for this person who I had previously been so resistant to. I had been looking for her to treat me with respect and understanding, but she was incapable of giving me those things. She was just acting the way she knew how, and it didn't have anything to do with me. I decided instead to focus on what I was gaining out of this experience. I got to be creative and sing and dance. I was having fun performing, and I was reaffirmed in my talents. From this place of gratitude for the opportunity to do what I loved, I was suddenly no longer at her whim. That was the most incredible and liberating moment. When we are fighting with someone, they have power over us, but when we accept a situation, we find a sense of liberation.

What was most interesting happened next. The director actually came to me and said, "Agapi, you don't have to clean so much! Please go with your friends. You have done an amazing job, and you are such a great actress." She just showered me with acknowledgment. The transformation that had taken place inside of me was beginning to manifest itself in my external world. I was stunned! My prayers were working beyond my wildest imagination.

If someone is not showing you the level of respect you deserve or is making it hard for you to do the work you know you're meant to do, bring that damaged part of yourself into the light and see what choices you have. You can take responsibility for the parts of yourself that you might be mistreating, pushing aside, or failing to honor and respect. I believe that the world reflects back to us the shadow parts of ourselves that we have left unexamined or unresolved. If we take full responsibility for the way people are treating us, which we are in some unconscious way allowing, then we will find that we have the power to choose differently, and miraculously the people around us will change. If you need to leave a situation, then leave, but know that the same thing might happen in the next job you take or in the next relationship you enter into. At some point, you might need to work out the pattern of being disrespected within yourself.

This prayer is for anyone who has felt hurt, dishonored, victimized, or disempowered. This can happen in a personal or professional relationship, but ultimately, we pray for the healing to happen within our own consciousness.

The Prayer

Dear Beloved,

I bring to you the part of me that feels discounted, hurt, or disrespected.

Please shed the light so that I may see where I have discounted, hurt, or disrespected myself.

I ask that the healing embrace of the spirit reach out to my human part that wants others to treat me in a loving and attentive way, that wants to be taken care of in the way I take care of others. I ask that my heart open to that part, and bring it understanding, sweetness, and even humor.

I ask that the light bridge the gap between what I am getting from others and what I want. I ask that grace be extended in the relationship in which I don't feel seen, so I can have distance from who they are and how they act toward me. I pray for courage in myself and the willingness to be neutral, not take anything personally, and not collapse within myself.

In truth, I want to know that no one can really hurt me unless I allow it.

I cannot control how other people act, but I do have

control over how I react. I ask for the inner support to bring that knowledge and wisdom to myself. I am free in my ability to control my own reaction.

Let the spirit in me help me move forward, suspend judgment, and expand into the field of forgiveness.

I also ask that I see the situation from a new perspective. I am not a victim, and no person has authority over me. I claim my inner authority, which is my God-given right.

I can keep my heart open and see how spirit and the light can help me transform the situation.

I hand it over to the higher light and I go free. That's what means the most to me—my freedom, my peace, my inner calm, and my unconditional love for myself.

So be it!

31

Resetting Your Balance

Have you ever started your day with good intentions, and then something happens that sets you off? You're on your way to work and the subways are delayed, or you're driving and get stuck in traffic, so you're late for an important meeting. Or you're getting ready to drop your kids off at school when your child spills his chocolate milk all over his new pants. Or you had wonderful plans for the weekend, and your friend calls to say she's come down with a cold and needs to cancel. Something happens that puts a damper on your day, and you don't have much time to process it because you have to get on to the next thing. Now you're carrying the emotional aftermath of the incident in a knot in your stomach, and you are completely distracted from whatever is coming next.

It is so important to find a few moments to reset your energy by taking some conscious breaths and returning to your center. This a very powerful tool that prevents your day from spiraling out of control. Often, the obstacle to resetting our energy in these moments is judging ourselves. We feel that we've done something wrong, or we blame ourselves for things that are beyond our control. We have an idea of how our day *should* go, but so many things can happen that do not match our expectations and we're thrown. If we approach things with too much rigidity, we become overly focused on what's not going according to plan and pull ourselves out of the moments of our lives. But when was the last time you actually had a day go according to your plan? Exercising your flexibility muscle is one of the greatest keys to having a good day.

I once had a situation at the airport when my flight to Los Angeles had been delayed until further notice. When I went up to the gate attendant and asked questions, the attendant got very frustrated and said, "Ma'am, we'll let you know when we know, but right now we know nothing," which was not very reassuring. I knew this was a time for me to call on the tool of prayer. I asked for guidance, peace, and creative solutions to my predicament. Within twenty minutes, I ran into someone I knew who had found another airline with a flight departing to Los Angeles in half an hour. I called right away and managed to get a seat on this flight. It was a rare occurrence when I only brought a carry-on and didn't need to deal with baggage. I believe taking that time to recenter and clear the negativity made all the difference.

Flexibility is the magic potion that unlocks the rigidity that we can fall into and the frustration we feel when things go the way they want to go, not the way we want them to go. If you can remain flexible, you will experience greater ease and more fun in every day. Your heart will be open and light, and when things go awry, as they inevitably will, you can pray for balance and renewal to return to your center. The gift of such flexibility is that you may receive guidance about what you need to do—and sometimes there is nothing to do. So, if you let go and anticipate your next opportunity, you will be in a state of acceptance and grace and, in that space, miracles can happen. Here is our prayer.

The Prayer

Dear Beloved,

I have just experienced a situation that threw me off balance, and I ask that I may forgive, clear, and disconnect from what just occurred.

I am upset and feel discomfort, and I ask that I take a moment to return to my quiet, allowing my heart to soften and to clear. I send love to myself, and I ask that I be guided toward anything specific I need to do to let it go.

I ask that all those who were involved be sent the light and positive energy. I remind myself of our oneness, and I ask that they, too, receive the blessing of a release.

I'm willing to let go and move on in order to embrace the rest of my day.

I return to the gratitude of the new moment, and as I receive my next breath, I ask that I come into my presence, my acceptance, and my joy.

I trust that there is joy and calm underneath the upset. As I stretch my flexibility muscle, I am grateful to know that I have the choice to let go of the disturbance right now. I breathe out my desire for control and I breathe in my acceptance of what is.

I thank you. I let my loving fill me. I set myself free. So be it.

32

Yes, You Can Kick the Worry Habit

I was brought up in a country where people have a lot of worries; there is a prevalent angst and anxiety that runs through my Greek culture. We even have famous Greek worry beads, which people play with endlessly to disperse the worry that they carry inside of them. In my early years, thank God, I found yoga and meditation, which helped me feel more centered, connected, and uplifted from the energies of anxiety and worry. Worry is a habit, and like any bad habit, we need to address and master it.

People who suffer from anxiety and worry have often created patterns of catastrophic thinking that forbids them from seeing positive outcomes. These become fixed neural pathways. Changing and reversing those pathways takes discipline, devotion, and regular practice. Sometimes, calmness is so far from your reality, it can sound like a foreign language. But becoming fluent in it will open you up to so much wisdom. If you asked me, "What's the one thing you wish for everyone, everywhere?" I would say, "I want people to move past their anxiety and worry into their calmness."

I am reminded of a friend of mine whose son had just returned from his first semester of college. She asked him how he was doing, and he told her, "Mom, I'm anxious all the time." She looked him in the eye and said, "Honey, you've got to get an inner life! Or life will be hell."

If you stay focused on the physical, material world all the time, you will suffer from anxiety and worry, and you will never feel calm. Unless you understand on a deep level that you are not just a body randomly thrown onto this earth, but that you are a soul with a destiny and a purpose, you will be filled with anxiety. Calmness comes from a deeper place, where you meet your inner source. When you enter that place, you put distance between you and your preoccupation with yourself. It is a quality that comes with practice, surrendering to the higher nature through meditation, conscious breathing, journaling to find out what is disturbing you, and calling yourself to be mindful and present at each moment.

It starts with the breath. When I feel anxious, I can feel

adrenaline pumping through my body, and I can't stand it. I have different techniques to get me out of that state as fast as I can. First, I give myself the mental direction to be steadier and take mental dominion over that lower energy. I ask to bring in more light. I never tell myself to stop worrying; instead, I give myself a substitute for the worry and evoke a different space of calmness. It's really about moving from the sympathetic to the parasympathetic nervous system. The sympathetic nervous system puts us into fight or flight mode and prepares our systems for defense, whereas the parasympathetic nervous system relaxes our body and invites more breath and spaciousness. You can make this shift with your breath, with calming music, or by intoning a mantra, like *hu,* which means "God" in Sanskrit, *ohm,* or simply chanting vowels aloud. Your diaphragm will release, and you'll breathe more oxygen into your body. Often, anxiety happens because we shut off our breath, and the brain feels deprived of oxygen. When we are feeling scared, it is hard to see the simple solutions available to us.

As you practice steadying, slowing, and deepening your breath, you enter a space that is heavenly. It reminds me of a saying my spiritual teacher uses: "Heaven is not a location, it's a vibration that we all have access to 24-7." I think of that reality and it shifts me to the realization that I can tap into that presence of the heavenly feeling.

The Prayer

Dear Beloved,

Let me attune myself to the deeper calmness and peace, to the higher vibration that is present in the universe, the cosmos, and everything that moves.

I ask to know that beyond the storms, the hurricanes, and the turbulence of the sea, there is a stillness and a calmness that is always present.

Show me that so much of my anxiety and worry comes from my personality and the humanness of this physical world. May I please know that I am rooted in the spirit, and experience its presence.

I see my roots being grounded in this earth and connecting to the heavens, so there is a convergence between my earthly self and my divine self. Although I may not know it or feel it, I claim it, and I allow it to be present and transform any conditions that I have placed between my soul and my worldly self that have caused me worry and anxiety.

I feel an invisible presence of steadiness walking with me every step of the way, and I start to feel the energy of peace so deeply. I hear the voice of wisdom inside of me whispering words of safety, trust, and direction, and I allow myself to attune my being to this frequency of calmness.

Anytime I bring worry upon myself, I remember that it's a product of the false self, and my true self only knows peace, calm, and serenity. In serenity, there are solutions, motivation, creativity, joy, and possibilities.

I do not give over to this worry. I do not give over to the anxiety and restlessness. I return to the invisible force inside of me that is enveloping me, embracing me, and cheering me on.

So be it!

33

When You Shut Others Out, You Shut Yourself Down

For a very long time, I walked through life feeling disconnected from myself. Although I was functioning in the world, working and pursuing my dreams, more often than not, I wasn't getting what I really wanted. And what I wanted was a connection to myself. As I did more inner work, it became clear that I needed to heal the wounded child within me and break my habit of comparing myself to others. As I opened up to my own love for myself, I started to connect with the girl in me who felt abandoned and discounted.

When my parents died three and a half months apart, I walked around feeling incredibly separate from everyone except my sister and two very close friends. I felt that people could not meet me in my grief. It just so happened that one of my close friends fell in love with her dream man around that time. She would call me, wanting to connect and share with me how wonderful she was feeling, but I was in such pain, so far removed from her experience at that time, that I completely avoided her. I couldn't express what I was feeling. I couldn't be vulnerable with her, so I withdrew. When we withdraw from others, we often withdraw from ourselves as well. We shut off our hearts, and it feels like something freezes inside of us.

Unresolved pain has a way of leading us to experiences that trigger that very same pain. Every time this happens, it's a new opportunity to heal. If a colleague is shutting you out or if you fear vulnerability, perhaps you have a fear of abandonment or a fear of exposure. Many of us have trouble being intimate with ourselves, meeting ourselves where our pain, discomfort, and true feelings are. So, we shut down. When we are shut down to ourselves, we close ourselves off from connections with others.

It took a while for me to reunite with that friend and bring the flow back into our relationship. At a time when she and her dream man had separated, and I had moved past the heavy grief

I was feeling, we were able to be together and openly express our past and present feelings about our lives. I had regained my connection to myself, which allowed me to recover my connection with her. It was the most beautiful healing, through which I realized that we can move through even the most difficult, painful experiences and get to the other side.

Here is the greatest key: if you are feeling separate from someone in your life—a coworker, ex-partner, lover, friend, or parent—explore the judgment you have of the other person as well as the judgment you have of yourself, so whether this person continues to be in your life or not, you can let any judgment go. If you are on the receiving end of someone icing you out, release any judgment you are imposing on yourself and embrace as much forgiveness as you can.

It all comes back to taking responsibility for yourself, owning your feelings, and knowing that, as you heal, the separation diminishes. Ask yourself often: What do I need to do to release myself from the judgment and the way I feel so I can return to my open heart? Allowing your love to flow freely is one of the greatest gifts you can give yourself and others. It's worth everything to open your heart to yourself and take yourself in.

So let us pray.

The Prayer

Dear Beloved,

I often walk through the world feeling disconnected and lost, as if I am looking for myself and don't know where to find me.

I ask now for the light of the spirit to protect me, fill me, and surround me, so that I may open my heart to a deeper connection with myself, embracing all parts of myself—my child self, my adult self, my longing self, my worrying self, my fearful self.

I ask that I may look at myself with the loving eyes of my soul so I can bring love, compassion, and awareness to my loneliness and give myself permission to express my old hurts, disappointments, and unfulfilled wishes. I ask that I may express them until I can let them go.

Help me find the one that knows how to comfort me, the spirit that is sweet and tender, and let it embrace me. Let me trust that I can experience my true self and know that I am enough and there is nothing wrong with me.

Remind me that in my human life, I am doing the best I can, and in this self-compassion, let me release my judgments of myself, my life, and the people around me who do not meet my expectations. Let me know that I can feel whole and complete, and still be in the process of unfolding, of becoming, and of knowing that the spirit lives in me.

Any blocks that I have placed in my mind, any doors that I have closed in my heart, let them be released with my next breath as I exhale, so that I can relax into the sweet connection with myself—nothing more, nothing less—simply being in true loving acceptance of all of me.

So be it.

V

Loving

34

The Gift of Praying for Others

At some point one's prayers will become
so powerful that they can shake a full tree
in an orchard in heaven and fruit will roll
through the streets in this world.
But, dear, until you can do that, maybe
apprentice yourself to someone who can,
and they will help your destiny achieve the
height of the extraordinary influence you
can yield.

—HAFIZ

Using prayer to help and bless someone else is one of the greatest gifts you can give. In praying for another, you can activate the God within you even more immediately than when you pray for yourself.

If you want to know the feeling of being loved, have someone else pray for you. There have been many instances in which others have prayed for me, and it has moved my heart and given me the ability to find my strength and my confidence during some hard times.

One of those times, I was with my spiritual teacher, John-Roger. We have a circle of friends on a shared spiritual path who gather for holidays and other special occasions. One year, we gathered in Los Angeles to celebrate New Year's Eve. One of our rituals for the New Year is to go around the dinner table and put our wishes forward into the shared energy of love and light. That night, when it was my teacher's turn to share his wishes, he started by praying for me. This took me by surprise, but it shouldn't have. I was going through a very difficult time in my life. I was living in New York, away from my sister, my mother, and my nieces, and I had begun working on a new book, but I was struggling with the project. I felt alone and stuck in my life.

When John-Roger prayed for me, he said, "Lord, I ask that you boost Agapi and give her the confidence to know her direction and her path. Bless her with joy and creativity and renew her enthusiasm for life." He went on to say, "For you know that she has faced difficulties and challenges. Where others would have turned stone cold, she has overcome." At that point, I began to cry, but they were tears of release and gratitude. I felt seen, acknowledged, and loved. I felt that I was not alone.

The profound power of that moment made an imprint on my consciousness that has stayed with me to this day. Moreover, my life completely changed after that evening. I returned to New York and everything began to align. Help came to me in many forms, and I was able to complete the book I was writing, *Conversations with the Goddesses,* as I tapped into and trusted my own creativity. I felt that I had rekindled my lifeline to the spirit and I felt the invisible support surrounding me and carrying me forward throughout my days. John-Roger's prayer and blessing planted seeds that took root and flourished as I cultivated them.

After that experience, I have never underestimated the power of our prayers to help us support one another, and I have tried to share this gift wherever and whenever I am able. Such a moment occurred when I was given the opportunity to pray for a new friend, Stephanie, who had joined me, my sister, and some friends for dinner at our home. That evening, Stephanie was distraught. She had been fired from her job as a journalist, she had just ended a long-term relationship, and she had no savings or safety net to fall back on. She was just forty-five, but she felt like her life was ending.

I asked Stephanie if she prayed. She looked at me as though I was speaking Greek. "Pray?" she asked me. "To whom?" I replied, "What about praying to the intelligence of the thirty-eight trillion cells that are making you right now?" She laughed. Then I suggested that we pray together. I took her hands, called in the light, and said aloud, "We ask for a blessing of renewal and strength and clarity for my friend Stephanie, so that she may renew her faith, her hope, and her trust in her ability to create new opportunities and form new relationships, to move into the knowing that she is not alone, and to have confidence in all that is possible for her." That was all it took. Stephanie began to cry and told me that nobody had ever done anything like that for her before. I told her that someone had done it for me, and I had learned that each human being, with their love and intention and good wishes, can help lift the consciousness and spirit of another.

Sure enough, I watched as Stephanie's life began to shift. Soon after that night, she got a new job. Over time, she began to put herself out there in an effort to meet new people. Now, she has a sense of confidence in herself, her gifts, and her path.

Our power to pray for one another is one of the surest ways to experience our inner abundance because when we see the gifts that we can offer others, we know the gifts that live within us.

The Prayer

Dear Beloved,

I ask that I may step out of my own way and may be used as a service to help my friend or this person find their strength, their inspiration, and their trust in life again as they see that they are not alone.

I ask that they release into the light any feelings of doubt, fear, worry, separation, hurt, or hopelessness, so they may be restored to knowing that they can rise again to a sense of wholeness, find their center, and discover a new direction in their life. Help this person open their consciousness and their vision so they may see new possibilities, new friends, new sources of support, and open their hearts to receive what is available to them.

I ask for this for the highest good so that they may restore themselves to their trust in the promise of their lives. May they experience support from within and without on their journey forward.

So be it.

35

Finding Your People

For most of my life, I have tried to find the place where I belong. Moving from Greece to London was a huge change. It took a lot of learning to adapt to a new culture with entirely different customs. When I came to America, I explored spiritual paths and looked for people to feel at home with. There were periods of my life when I felt like I had found them, and there were periods when I felt very alone and separate from the world around me.

One of the most wonderful experiences is finding people you can share life with, who become lifelong friends. You can share your challenges and your successes, difficult moments, little victories, and the times when you feel you are growing. Those types of friendships can make life so rich. When I first moved to Los Angeles to work as an actor, I was invited by a Hollywood producer to audition for a movie. Through that experience, I met a tremendous number of people. Because of my nature and how "Greekarious" I am, I was able to become very socially connected. But I was missing the closeness that I felt with my family, my mother, my sister, my friends, and my community in London. It was the vastness of the city of Los Angeles, with so many people from all over, that made me feel there was no center, no community. I was constantly meeting new people, but it was very difficult for me to find people I could open up to and become friends with. There is nothing worse than knowing a lot of people but feeling like no one really knows you. It creates incredible feelings of loneliness and isolation, like something is amiss.

A few months into my stay in Los Angeles, the movie I had moved there to do fell through. But, right around that time, I was introduced to a spiritual teacher, John-Roger, in whom I found a mentor and way-shower. I also joined a wonderful spiritual community that made me feel more connected and at home. Even though the movie had fallen through, I decided to stay and focus on my spiritual path. I got into a relationship with a lovely man whom I felt at home with, and I started to become very discerning of who my real friends were. I let go of a lot of the social engagements that made me feel empty, and I concentrated on the few people who I felt very close to and who I could be myself with. Little by little, I started to distinguish between the people who were going to be part of my tribe and the people who were going to be acquaintances.

Sharing yourself authentically is the greatest way to find who your people are. The more we open up to ourselves, the more committed we become to knowing who we truly are, what makes us happy, and what makes us feel alive and joyful. As we get to know ourselves better, we get better at finding other people who we can authentically connect with. I started to discover my uniqueness and how my energy, heart, personality, and gifts were adding to other people's lives, and that gave me a sense of confidence to share more of who I was. Just know, no matter where you are and no matter how you are feeling, the greatest key to finding your people is knowing how much you can add to people's lives. You'll need to affirm your worthiness and risk being open. If you are closed off, always expecting other people to first reach out to you, it's going to be very hard to find your people.

The more I trusted my ability to reach out and connect in a heartfelt way, the more I was able to experience deep and fulfilling friendships. Here are my five important tips for finding your people:

1. Be generous.
2. Be discerning.
3. Be open.
4. Put up your friendship antenna so you will attract the people who are right for you.
5. Trust that you can and deserve to have amazing friendships and connections with people who care for you. See your value as you see the value in others.

The Prayer

Dear Beloved,

I ask that I may become more aware of my spirit's aliveness within me. My human part feels separate and disconnected from the people I meet, and I long for the connection of friendship. I want to find my tribe—the people I resonate with—so I can experience sharing the joys of life with them in an authentic and open way, with no pretense but with a light heart.

I ask that I may open myself to receiving these people into my life now and that I may be shown how to find them.

I ask that the sweetness and tenderness that I crave in real companionship find me. Let me open the door to any new opportunities. I now see that happening in all parts of my life—at work, at the coffee shop, in a class at the gym, or at an event where I don't know many people. I see myself creating deep friendships and intimate relationships. I allow myself to share more of who I am as I meet good people through grace.

I see this as a positive way to experience my fullness and aliveness. I see this happening in the perfect way and in the perfect time. I let go of any old beliefs and limitations that keep me separate from others.

Guide me to the ways that I can be my own best friend. Guide me to know that I can enjoy my own company, know more of who I am, and deepen my connection with myself. May I know that you are always with me, loving me, and that the spiritual beings that work with me in the invisible world are assisting me in every part of my life.

As I create a warm sense of home inside of me, I see that reflected in my physical world. I receive the magic of that feeling of belonging within myself, and then meet my people, whom I can enjoy sharing my life with.

So be it!

Prayer for a Blessed Marriage

Dear Beloved,

We first thank the spirit for bringing these two people together to love, honor, and cherish each other.

We ask right now for a blessing to be placed on them, a blessing of joy. As they see each other every morning and come back home every night from wherever they have been, they will feel the joy of having found each other and remember how love brought them together. Let this love be ignited so that it will carry them through any adversities or challenges in their lives.

We ask for them to affirm their joy and have courage as they grow to communicate their honest feelings and trust that they will create a safe space for each other. We see their love in their hearts being amplified, and it will always be there to lift them up together.

In the face of any disagreements between them over life decisions or desires, we ask that they may be wise and bring the greater presence of God to guide them and support them so they can come to the decisions about their lives together in one accord—to make nothing more important than love, harmony, and laughter.

May you know that this love that is charged here by the spirit of God will always be there to carry you forward through any adversities. Nurture it by doing little things every day to take care of each other. Keep your marriage spontaneous and alive, and never take each other for granted.

Celebrate your uniqueness, remembering that your complementary differences are what brought you together.

So let the spark of your joyful souls be expressed here today, and turn to this spark often to remind you of who you truly are together—of the light and force of love that is within you. Follow the light of your souls daily and trust that it will carry you forward to your life's expansion and fulfillment. May you be showered with God's abundant blessings in every aspect of your life together.

36

To Compare Is to Despair

I do not try to dance better than anyone else.
I only try to dance better than myself.
—Mikhail Baryshnikov

Comparison has been one of my lifelong patterns. I felt so consumed by it when I was younger that I didn't even recognize it as a thought pattern. As an actor, I would compare myself to other women in my field who seemed to be more successful, better known, and more confident than I was. Those women always seemed to land the roles. Because I so longed to become a well-known actor, I compared myself to every actor who received more recognition than I did. As if that wasn't bad enough, I would then judge myself for comparing myself to others.

I was once at the gym with my niece when I saw a book by an author I had been comparing myself to, whose sales figures were higher and social media following much larger than mine. My niece and I chuckled. She said to me, "Well, here it is to make sure you get triggered again so that you can get over it once and for all." The world has a way of pulling us into a mindset in which we are solely focused on external success. I knew that being triggered by seeing a fellow author's book was a test of how anchored I was in my sense of self, my sense of value, and my sense of my own worthiness beyond external measurements. When we feel a sense of internal lack, we imagine that other people have what we believe we are missing, but it's an illusion.

The energy running underneath comparison is really a sense of lack, feeling "less than." It's something that runs wild in our society and destroys our sense of self, joy, and confidence. So many young people suffer from this pattern, especially in relation to social media. People always look fabulous on social media, like they're having the best time, but you don't know what is happening when they turn their cameras off. Whatever you imagine is happening in their lives is really a projection of what you feel that you are lacking.

Trace the pattern of comparison to its beginning. Are you possibly addicted to feeling bad about yourself? Ask yourself: When did it start? Who did I inherit this from? What was the incident in my childhood or young life that triggered it? Comparison is a deeply rooted seed of lack. Address it at its core and begin to unwind it by using the pattern of comparison as your teacher. Be honest with yourself: What would you like more of in your life? What experience are you looking to have? Describe it to yourself in detail and look for ways to incorporate elements of what you want into your life right now. You need to fuel yourself with positive affirmations, fill yourself up with a sense of worthiness and value, and learn to love and accept yourself without conditions. Instead of feeling deflated by what you perceive others have, be inspired by what you can become. Your path is uniquely carved out and it is uniquely yours. To compare yourself to others is to cheat yourself of the gifts you possess and the opportunity to live a fuller life.

I love the quote from the spiritual teacher Macrina Wiederkehr: "O God, help me believe the truth about myself, no matter how beautiful it is." It takes courage to see our own beauty, face our own light, and experience our own lovability, to fully receive who we are. So let us pray that we can move into our peace and find our uniqueness.

The Prayer

Dear Beloved,

I am very aware of a pattern that no longer serves me. I look at others and feel I fall short. I give my power away to what other people have and what I perceive they are experiencing in life, and I make myself less. I feel a sense of lack in myself and in my life.

I feel as if others have qualities and abilities that make them far more competent than I am. It comes in so many forms, and I start to feel bad about myself.

Although I may want and desire more things, I ask to find peace with the fact that my path is a commitment to knowing myself, appreciating my life, and serving others with the wisdom gained from my life's experiences.

I ask that I let go and surrender any attachment to what other people have or do, and see how I might be able to bring more of my expression and joy into the world. Help me know that my intimate relationship with you is where I can feel the expansion of myself. In my relationship with spirit, my life can be amplified and directed. Help me trust that the light will show me opportunities to enrich my life.

When the pattern of comparison comes, instead of judging it, let me observe it as something of the magnetic material world that can suck me in. Let me rise to my mighty spirit and know that the material world has no power over me. I do not allow this lesser energy to diminish me in any way or form. I am done with it. I am really done with it. With spirit on my side, I release it completely and I go free.

Help me see my life with the eyes of gratitude so I may open up to receive.

I thank you with all my heart. What a gift my life is. So be it!

Prayer for Letting Go of Conflict

Dear Beloved,

I am willing to move forward. The past events that disturbed me are still lodged in my thoughts and belly. They are festering in my consciousness, and I want to let go of what happened, but I'm feeling stuck and can't seem to do that.

Like an anchor, the feelings and the judgments are pulling me back into the deep, and I want to return to the shore, clear and free.

I am willing to move in the present and bring my presence to the part of me that hurts and is ruminating in the old.

I feel like I can't control the situation or this person; I would like them to act differently, yet I have no power over what they do.

I get triggered, so I ask that I can move into acceptance.

As it is with any fruit tree in any garden, some fruits are ripe for the picking, some are still ripening, and some are not ready to pick yet. Some are so high I cannot reach them, and some are within arm's reach. So it is with people. I cannot rush the ripening.

Let me now accept this, and if I can, let me allow what I don't agree with to exist without making the other person wrong.

If I can, let me reach upward and inward and extend the ray of loving to them inwardly—the ray of loving I know in my heart so well, the ray of peace, and the ray of the uplifting spirit that exists to make all things fall into place.

So this, too—this relationship, this event—now falls into the perfect place in the order of all things. If there is any other piece of wisdom that can be awakened in my consciousness, I allow myself to hear it in my heart so I *may hear the whisper of guidance instead of the noise of my limited personal opinions, thoughts, and judgments. Help me move these conditions into the unconditional nature of love.*

So be it.

37

Free Yourself from Being Caught in the Middle

Some time ago, two dear friends of mine got into an argument about a business deal. They both believed that they were entitled to a greater share of the profits and they couldn't come to an agreement. Harsh words were exchanged and they each held on to their position and their anger. Because I was close to both of them, they each confided in me, telling me how they felt about the other, how hurt they were, and who was right and who was wrong. It's very difficult to be caught in the middle of an argument between colleagues, couples, or friends. I often find myself being Switzerland in a situation of conflict, perhaps because I am averse to conflict, since it goes against my belief in an ideal utopic world where everyone loves one another and gets along.

Maybe I need to resolve something inside myself to know that conflict is a part of life.

With my two friends, I found myself ruminating over who was right and who was wrong as I tried to figure out what I could do as a neutral party. It was not really my conflict to resolve, so I tried to stay outside of the discord and disturbance that they were both experiencing. Since then, I have found some effective ways to deal with this sort of situation. I have found that the best approach is to pray about holding a neutral position and becoming a positive presence for the people who are suffering from the disturbance.

The greatest challenge is to not judge the situation. The truth is, you don't really know what those two people are working through. There was a time when I lived with a couple, and they were constantly arguing and making up. Whenever they would argue, she would come to me and say how hard it was for her, how he drove her crazy, and she couldn't stand it anymore. He would lie to her, and she couldn't trust him, so I would try to fix it and tell her what to do. Well, a day or two later they would make up and return to enjoying themselves, but I would still be engulfed in the upset! Eventually, I moved out because their dynamic was too exhausting for me to live with.

Similarly, when I was performing in a play, two of the actors were in conflict and kept bringing it up to the director and the rest of the cast. It was disturbing to everybody. They were trying to tell each other how to act, and whatever one was doing, the other said it was not working. The play was supposed to be a comedy, but it was turning into a tragedy. One day, in the middle of rehearsal, the director said to them, "Please, go find a coffee shop and work this out, and if you don't, I will let go of both of you because it's affecting the whole cast. Don't come back until it is worked out." And they worked it out. I think that was a very wise way for the director to deal with the situation. It's very liberating to know that we don't always have to be the one who is bringing peace to the conflict. We can hand it right back to its creators and say, "Hey, you have all the tools inside of you to deal with this. I can be a sounding board and listen to you, but ultimately you're the ones who need to resolve this."

The truth is, we don't really know what two people have come together to work out, what lessons they need to learn and what awareness they need to gain. Many lessons can be learned from conflict—how to assert yourself, when to back off, how to practice patience. A conflict can be an important opportunity for a person to address an obstacle in their life on a spiritual level. They might need to learn how to set aside their egos and communicate in a heartfelt way. Or they might be learning how to use their voices. If you interfere in a conflict that isn't yours, you may prevent these lessons from being learned. If you do find yourself in the middle of a conflict that is not your own, holding a higher consciousness of loving and resolution is the most valuable thing you can do for all parties involved. So let us pray!

The Prayer

Dear Beloved,

I come present in my heart, and I bring this situation into the light.

> *I am witnessing a disagreement between two people I care for, and although I am feeling the disturbance in my heart, I ask that I be given the strength and wisdom to remove myself from the situation, refrain from taking sides or internalizing the hurt that they might have caused each other, and extend the higher light to them as I disconnect myself from the conflict.*

> *As those two individuals confide in me or share their issues and judgments of each other, I ask that I set boundaries for how much I take in and how much I engage. Most of all, I protect myself from the discordant and unbalanced energy that they're experiencing and hold a consciousness of peace for all.*

I ask that a bridge of love, wisdom, and clarity be placed between me and them. I see these two people, in their highest good, returning to balance. Whether they decide to stay together or move apart, peace is present.

I thank you for allowing me to be the witness, and I humbly ask that you allow me to be a peacemaker for them without having to say too much or take sides. Let me hold my consciousness as a vessel of peace and love.

I send light to both of them, and I ask that, in the right time, they may return to a peaceful place in their hearts. I release any attachments to the outcome. I set them free and I go free.

So be it!

38

How to Lose an Argument and Still Be Okay

Perhaps it's not surprising that my story about an argument begins at the DMV.

Some time ago, I went to the DMV to take the written test to renew my driver's license, and when I gave it to the woman behind the counter, she told me that I needed another form that no one had told me about. In this situation, I explained to her that I didn't have that form because it was never sent to me, but she contradicted me and said that I should have received it. We got into a little bit of back and forth. I always get triggered by authority figures, so instead of being more cooperative with her, I kept protesting. Ultimately, she failed me and told me to come back another time to retake the test. I was furious and upset, but there was nothing I could do; if I wanted my license, I had to come back and do what she said. It would have been a wiser choice to recognize that there was no way I was going to win in this situation and to be humble in allowing her to wield the authority that, in this circumstance, she possessed. When I left, I was extremely upset, but there was nothing I could do. I needed my license, so I had to follow the rules and come back another time.

So often, when we get into an argument, our ego reacts. We want to get our way, no matter what. When we don't, we clash with whomever is standing in our way. It can get ugly. Sometimes we even say things that we regret later. It can happen with a significant other, a parent, a child, a colleague, a partner, or an airline agent. Most of us don't know how to lose an argument. We want to hold on to our position in order to prove that we are right, so we double down. You know what—you might be right! But if you are in a situation in which the other person isn't coming around, and you keep defending your position, you're going to feel the repercussions, especially if you use words with the objective to hurt the other person.

The only way out of the heartbreak of a disagreement is to apologize and to forgive. Often, after we have lashed out or snapped, we experience a backlash of self-criticism for losing our temper or being stubborn, and we hold on to that judgment against ourselves. So how do you return to your balance after you have an argument, so it doesn't ruin your day or your relationship? That's where prayer comes in. Prayer moves us into forgiveness and expansion so that our inner wisdom can assist us in letting go of our ego position and return us to a centered, heartfelt place out of which miracles can happen.

After the situation at the DMV, I prayed and forgave myself. I saw that I had asserted my ego too much and failed to use my wisdom: in that moment, having the humility to make an apology would have worked to my advantage. I asked for the light to assist me in returning to my center and using that experience as a lesson in awareness and discernment—when it's better to say nothing and to hold my peace.

My mother taught me how a smile and a good disposition goes a long way. Sharing your humanness and light can actually help you get the results you want. It's a form of prayer in the moment. In retrospect, when the DMV employee started to become combative, I should have accessed my wisdom to call on my higher guidance. I might have prayed to back off and bring the right attitude to the situation. For instance, I could have prayed, "I need help right now. There is a combative energy coming toward me, and I can feel it. Help me not combat it but hold my peace and let that energy dissipate." Had I done that, I might have turned the situation around. Or maybe not! But I would have maintained my calm and I could have left knowing I had done the best I could.

Accessing the power of prayer in the moment of conflict and sending the light to the other person can be so incredibly powerful and transformative. I refer to that DMV conflict whenever another person tries to exert power over me. It's almost like an alarm rings in my brain, saying, "Remember the DMV lady; start praying!" We can use painful situations as an example for the next time. These are the kinds of things you cannot learn from books or lectures, only from experience.

The Prayer

Dear Beloved,

I ask for the inner light to protect me, fill me, and surround me. I bring in the light, and I exhale my fears and my judgment. I ask to be receptive to guidance and direction.

In this particular situation, I ask that I may forgive myself for losing my cool—speaking out, lashing out, losing my temper, or snapping—and I ask that I may restore myself to peace, calm, and balance.

I ask right now that I may let go of any anger or animosity toward this person and that I may deflect any hostility that is coming toward me, so I may be released from the cycle of negativity.

If I need to apologize to the person and ask them for their forgiveness, let me find the humility to do so.

I ask that I may also forgive them for how they acted and let go of the judgments that I have toward them.

I ask that I may again come into balance with this person within myself and return to my intention to always communicate with love and compassion.

I now place this situation into the higher light, and I ask that any negativity be diffused and dispersed. In its place may I see grace, upliftment, and serenity. In the vortex of that new energy, I let myself be spirit-led in my communication so that I may see a complete resolution of this situation. I am grateful and filled with peace.

So be it!

39

Breaking the Pattern of Unhealthy Attachments

I've been there. You know—the feeling of a relationship that takes you over and under and makes you feel like you lost yourself. I'm grateful I went through it, and I'm grateful I'm out of it now. When a romantic relationship takes over your life, you can become consumed by the relationship. You can't stop thinking about the other person, and your well-being depends on how they react to you. You want them to love you more than anything, and you want them to be open to your love for them. You basically want "the full monty!"

There was a time in my life that I haven't wanted to relive, and I haven't even wanted to write about, because it was so painful. I feel ashamed, even now, that I was at the whim of someone else's behavior, and I didn't know how to pull myself back from the ledge. I love the feeling of falling in love and the exquisite experience of being in love. A person in love seems to glow; they are more radiant and they feel a fullness inside. But in this case, I found that my identity was entirely defined by my relationship to that person. It was god-awful! That kind of attraction is more of addiction than love. I remember praying so much during that time. At first I prayed for his attention and affection, but over time I began to pray for my freedom.

What made this particular relationship so hard was that, in truth, he was very inconsistent. He would show up, and we would have a wonderful time together, and then he would disappear, so I was always left in limbo, unable to function. When he was not there, my thoughts and emotions revolved around him—missing him, wanting him, not knowing how to fix the relationship, and not knowing how to let go. I felt powerless in his presence and paralyzed to speak my truth to him out of fear that he would leave.

When we don't have a full sense of ourselves and haven't developed into who we are, the attention of and the attraction to another human being makes us feel a sense of self. We attach to that feeling and that person, and we call it love. When that feeling goes away or collapses, or the person leaves, we are then left with the empty shell of ourselves because we haven't yet filled ourselves with our own being. Being so attached to another person in a romantic relationship is like being an alcoholic: you have no control. To heal, you have to give yourself over to a higher power. You have to admit that you've become addicted to that person's energy, and you have to go through the process of surrendering if you want to receive help.

For me, it took a few blows and experiences that were so excruciatingly painful before, one day, I was on my knees praying, "Please, God, take this away from me." I was weeping and crying, and I heard a voice inside of me, as clear as a bell, saying, "We will help you, but you can never have sex with him again." Sexual engagement reinforces the attachment. I would try to disconnect, but then we would engage sexually and I would reattach. So, I began weaning myself off this person. I kept a diary and logged every day that I would not call or reach out. When he reached out, I would not respond. Every time I made the choice to not connect with him was a win. It felt like shedding a skin; every fiber of my physical, emotional, and mental body was letting go. It was painful, but my soul was rejoicing in reclaiming my energy.

They say thirty-two days is how long it takes to institute a new behavior pattern in your brain. Those first thirty-two days led to another thirty-two days, and another thirty-two days, and day by day, month by month, I was gaining my freedom. It was like walking back onto the shore from the depths of the ocean. Exactly a year later, I had a birthday and was celebrating with my friends when somebody asked me, "What was the best thing that happened to you this year?" Without hesitation, I replied, "I am now free of this person and the emotional addiction. They are becoming a faint memory in my mind, and every day they are receding further in my consciousness. I am so grateful." It reminds me of the song by Taylor Swift, "I Forgot That You Existed." I guess she went through it as well!

That is the power of spiritual help, my friends, along with my own cooperation with myself. I had to ask, surrender, and be willing to let go, and then the help came! I have not experienced pain like that since. I feel that I broke through an addictive attachment to another person. I write this prayer for anyone who is experiencing the all-consuming dependency on another in a romantic relationship. If you are experiencing something that's not working for you, know that there is freedom on the other side if you allow yourself to ask and receive the help. Always remember that the most fulfilling relationship is the one you can cultivate with your own spirit.

The Prayer

Dear Beloved,

I center myself and I ask for the loving presence of the one that is with me and is there for me 24-7.

I've hit a rock and a hard place at the same time. Every fiber of my being is connected to and preoccupied by this person. I am at their whim; whether they will call me or reach out, how they will act when we are together, when they will come to spend time with me, when they will leave again, and what they will or won't say to me. I am completely under their spell.

I have lost every sense of myself, or the self I've known thus far.

Once I thought I found true love, everything was ignited in me. I was overjoyed, but now I know that this relationship is not working for me. It brings me down.

I need to disengage in order to return to myself, but I have no idea how to even begin to do that. All I know is I want to experience something other than what I am experiencing right now, which is beneath my spirit. I've been pulled too far away from shore, and I am in the deep end.

Guide me to a place where I can restore my wholeness, a

place where there is comfort, peace, and trust, where I can live without this person and be more than okay—happier, freer, and fuller.

I need a lifeline. I'm asking for a hand to bring me back onto the shore. I am willing to let go of this person and know that I can thrive without them and see the light again.

Show me how to shift my focus from them. Show me how to shift my attention. Allow me to drop any blame of myself for the choices I've made and trust that, by letting go of this person, I am doing the right thing for my well-being.

Fill the empty space with strength, renewed hope, and freedom from the chains of affliction in an addictive relationship.

Restore me to myself. Restore me to my love, my fulfillment, and the promise that I do not have to suffer anymore.

So be it.

40

Breaking Up: A Divine Opportunity to Upgrade Yourself

We've all suffered our share of breakups—some of them drag on until the final breakup happens, and others are an unexpected surprise, like the famous Post-it breakup between Berger and Carrie in *Sex and the City*. A breakup is life interrupted. We are heading one way, thinking we know the destination, with a mental image of how the future's going to look with this person in it, when suddenly we are confronted with the fact that this relationship is not going to go the distance. We have to reimagine the future. The devastation that we suffer very much depends on how invested we have been in the relationship.

The daughter of a dear friend of mine was engaged, and six months before the wedding date, she didn't feel quite right. She told her fiancé that she wasn't feeling sure about moving forward, and she called off the wedding. She was devastated and went through tremendous turmoil over whether she'd done the right thing. She had already chosen her wedding gown, had (obviously) to give back the ring, and felt she was facing the abyss of uncertainty.

Another friend of mine, a divorced mother of a young girl, was dating a man in another state for thirty years, back and forth. Their long-distance relationship was working very well, and he asked her to relocate with her daughter and move in with him. She agreed and moved across the country, only to discover a month later that her daughter didn't like him, he didn't like her daughter, and he wasn't what he had seemed when their relationship was bicoastal. She was devastated and found herself in a new city with no friends, working remotely with a young teenage daughter, completely distraught. She confessed to me that she was on the verge of a nervous breakdown because of the huge letdown. Yet she moved out, and a few months later, she moved to a place where there was a community available to her—she made friends, met colleagues, and felt supported. Being in a completely new environment started to restore her to herself, and over time, she learned that she had the strength to overcome such an immense disappointment and bring herself back to sanity. What a victory!

When I came to New York, I dated a man I thought was "the one"—at least, I had decided he was "the one." He had many qualities I was looking for in a man, and he also had feelings for me—so I ran with the initial excitement without seeing the whole picture. I projected onto him what I wanted to see, and when I saw who he really was, the breakup was inevitable. It was similar for my friend's daughter whose marriage fell apart. She, too, had projected onto her fiancé what she wanted to see and when she woke up from the illusion, she realized that she couldn't see a future with him. A year later, after she went through hell, depression, and tremendous guilt, she found the man for her—a wonderful man she loves who loves her back. They are a perfect match. If she had not found the courage to be honest in her previous relationship, she never would have known the happiness she now has in her life.

As hard as it can be, every breakup is an opportunity to get closer to what we truly want. When I talk to people who have been through terrible breakups, after some time has passed, they all say it was the best thing that ever happened to them. I can honestly tell you, I thank God I didn't marry any of the men I thought I wanted to marry!

This prayer will empower you to find the courage and the strength to let go and discover the wisdom and the purpose of why a relationship unfolds the way it does. This prayer is for anyone who has experienced a breakup, is in the middle of a breakup, or knows someone who is going through a breakup, to allow the light of the spirit to walk with you through this tunnel. As one of my favorite quotes says, "There is no light at the end of the tunnel. You are the light in the tunnel."

The Prayer

Dear Beloved,

My world has been shut down. This relationship that I've invested so much in, that I've hoped would be a happy relationship, has ended.

This ending for me right now is devastating. I don't know if I have it in me to go on. I cry, I hurt, and I feel like my heart is broken and bruised.

How do I heal? How do I restore? How do I trust that time is my friend and I will regain my joy and trust in love and intimacy?

I hear the voice of love inside that tells me to breathe deeply; I'm alive and well and I trust that I will come out of this. I will overcome. The relationship broke, but I am not broken. I forgive myself for any judgments I have about the situation, this person, and myself.

So I breathe—I breathe the spirit that's in me; I breathe it right now. I feel the embrace of love holding me and my broken heart, and I begin to feel more comforted and soothed.

Give me faith, give me hope, give me the light.

I kneel, hold myself, and take moments every day to feel the presence I know is in me, loving me—even when I do not feel it. I hold, I listen, and I let you love me.

So be it!

Quick God Fix for Finding the Courage to End a Relationship That's Not Working

God, make your magic happen so that breaking up with this person is grace-filled. Let me trust that the pain will subside so that we can both move on with compassion and acceptance.

41

Yes, You Can Be Happy After Divorce

I got married when I was very young, a few years after I moved from London to Los Angeles to embark on my acting career. My marriage was mostly about comfort and safety while I was living in an unknown and unpredictable world. The relationship was not a big romance or passion, but I felt safe and protected. A few years later, when it was apparent that I needed to move on in my own way, we first went through a separation, and then we went through the formality of a divorce. It was easier for me than for him, but it all worked out and we both moved on.

While I didn't personally have to process any big emotions, I have known so many couples whose divorces were excruciatingly difficult and hostile, with anger surfacing on both sides. There are many dynamics at play in a couple's unraveling—kids, intertwined finances, deceit, lying, unfaithfulness. Sometimes, two people simply grow apart.

I remember a friend of mine whose husband had a prominent job and was involved in an extramarital affair. He asked her for a divorce. They had kids, there was money involved, and they were in and out of court trying to work through appeals, child custody issues, and their financial settlement. My friend was in excruciating pain over this betrayal, and she couldn't get past it. This was somebody she loved, with whom she had three children, whose career she had loyally supported, and above all, to whom she had given her heart.

One day I invited her to walk the labyrinth in my spiritual center. As previously mentioned, this is a beautiful ancient tradition in which you set an intention or come up with a question you want an answer to, and with that in mind, you walk the labyrinth. It is a metaphor for the journey to the center of your deepest self and then back out into the world with a broadened understanding of who you are. She was going to court the next day, determined to fight to get as much money as she could.

Before she entered the labyrinth, she prayed to heal the pain her heart was experiencing. I sat on the side and meditated while she was walking the labyrinth. When she came out of it, there were tears running down her face, and she said to me, "I had the most extraordinary experience! When I was at the center of the labyrinth, I saw my ex-husband's soul beaming at me, and I felt this love that I had for him, for his soul, for who he is—the father of my children—and something in me just completely let go. I felt at peace. I felt that whatever he gives me, I will take. I felt complete, and I felt this grace relieve me from the anger that was exhausting me."

I cannot explain the joy I felt in my heart. To me, that was God in action. My friend went to court the next day and said to her lawyer, "I'm not fighting anymore. Whatever he gives me, he gives me." Her lawyer looked at her and asked, "Are you okay?" She said, "I am more than okay; I am free."

So, for anyone who is going through a difficult divorce, this prayer reassures you that with God as your partner, you can move toward freedom, you can rediscover peace. You don't have to be consumed by the anger and hostility of who is right and who is wrong. Divorce is never easy, but with the higher power on your side, it can be filled with forgiveness and grace. Here is a prayer that you can edit and embellish to match your specific circumstances.

The Prayer

Dear Beloved,

After years of being married to this person, the reality is that we have grown apart. There are many reasons, and a lot of them are so beyond me.

I am filled with disappointment, a sense of failure, and hurt, and I am overwhelmed with not knowing what the future holds. Everything looks bleak and uncertain, and now we are heading for divorce.

I blame myself and ask, "Where did I go wrong?" There may be hostility and there may be anger, but there are also two frozen hearts that feel broken.

It's surely too painful to live like this, even for one more day.

Right now, I ask to move into a higher altitude, to bring all my feelings to the table and find compassion for our humanness. I accept that two people can grow apart.

When I look back on the life we shared, let me remind myself of the good things that happened. Perhaps we have children together or built a beautiful home for our family or pushed each other to grow in important ways.

Give me the gift of transformation, so that the barren

areas of our lives transform to match the richness of our souls. With the light, I can come out of this tunnel as a winner rather than a loser. I do not need to see this experience as a failure, but rather as the destiny that I have fulfilled to gain greater awareness, wisdom, understanding, and humanity.

I ask for trust to know that every day is a step forward.

I anchor myself in this trust, this peace, this knowing that the one that walks in me and with me is bigger—wiser, more benevolent, more loving—than the one that is taking over my being in my worldly affairs.

Now, I turn my eyes inward and partner with my higher wisdom, my higher self, remembering that God is my partner. I take a moment now to let that reality infuse my being and show me that I can get through this divorce and keep my heart open. I don't have to give in to hatred, jealousy, or hostility.

I allow myself to feel vulnerable, tender, loving, and I know I am at home in my soul. That's all any of us can ask for: to walk through our human journey with the awareness of the light of our souls.

I'm thankful for this moment, and I will often return to it until it is done.

So be it.

Prayer for Anyone Planning to Start a Family

Dear Beloved,

My partner and I have decided to start a family.

It is a huge decision for us because we have enjoyed our independence in our lives together, and we understand the commitment and responsibility that comes with bringing a child into the world.

We ask now for a blessing that we may create a safe haven for the soul of this child as they join our family. We ask for the blessing of the divine light so that we may prepare ourselves with joy and trust and the belief that we can handle this, so that the resources will be there. Most of all, we ask that we have the inner resources to meet this challenge.

Please guide us in this adventure and allow any fear or trepidation to be dissolved so that we may feel only peace, joy, and the excitement of bringing a human being into the world.

With our gratitude and humility, so be it.

Prayer for a Mother Preparing for Birth

Dear Beloved,

For this gift of preparing my womb and body to give birth, I ask that this miracle of life bless every part of my body and the life that is forming in me.

I ask that any thoughts of fear, anxiety, or worry be transmuted into the trust and acceptance of what is to be, and I ask that I may be moved into the deepest, calmest place in my heart to allow this child to grow and be nourished in my womb.

I see the baby filled with health and a radiant light that helps it grow in perfection, and I flood my womb and my body with so much love, awe, respect, and reverence for that which is happening.

I let the joy of the prospect of becoming a mother fill my whole being.

I ask that I am open to receive any support that comes my way.

Most of all, I ask to listen inside to the soul of this child and what it needs every day. I ask, and I receive, and I allow moments of stillness and presence to know that beyond this body forming in my womb, the soul is waiting patiently to enter the body and come into this world. May I know this soul, and may I connect with it and listen to its presence, and may it become a love affair that will materialize and develop as this child is born.

Give me patience, understanding, respect, and love for myself and what my body and self are going through in this transformation. Let my tenderness for myself be equal to the tenderness that I have for this child, and let this tenderness lead my way to its birth, and continue on for years to come.

Although I cannot predict what this journey will be as this child is born, let me delight in the unknown and surprise of each day, watching the miracle of life in the form of this child becoming a human being.

I am so grateful. I am so thankful. I am filled with peace and bliss for this gift of life. So be it!

PS: And by the way, please also help me with my nausea and my cravings!

42

Parenting Through the Ups and Downs of the Teenage Years

I was having dinner with a dear friend of mine when he got a call from his ex-wife, who said that their son had been stopped by the police because one of his taillights was broken, and they found a vape pen in his car. The police were holding him at the station. My friend then told me that this had been a recurring theme in his son's life. He'd gotten involved with other kids who were vaping, was not being diligent with his studies, and was basically rebelling and slacking off. My friend and his ex-wife had given him notice many times, but his behavior remained the same. They cut off his allowance, took the car, and forbade him to go out with his friends, but nothing they said or did made a difference. My friend didn't know what to do next.

We decided, right then and there, to pray for his son, and we came up with this prayer to ask for the light to be with my friend and his son and guide them to find a new way to deal with this situation. Parents often don't know what to do with their teenage sons and daughters. Bringing spirit into the solution and asking other people to pray for your children or your friends' children is a very powerful means of support. Those teens might be having a karmically difficult time—they might be struggling because they don't know who they are. They might try everything to test the limits or to feel some kind of connection. They don't yet have the wisdom to make the best choices.

I've seen miracles happen when a group comes together to pray for a teenage son or daughter. My friend prayed and continues to pray, and many of us prayed for him and his son and held a positive vision of his well-being in our minds and hearts. A few weeks after that dinner, my friend told me they had found a wonderful therapist who was able to get through to the son. The therapist helped him connect to what he loved to do and clarify how he saw himself in his future. He shared with the therapist that he dreamed of playing music with a band and eventually moving out of his parents' home. She helped him connect to a sense of purpose in his life and understand that if he was giving up on himself, by not studying and always getting in trouble, he would not be able to realize his dreams.

When we give kids a vision of where they can go, we help them connect to their dreams and to what makes them feel alive and expressive. Punishing them is not going to do this. It requires tremendous skill to reach these kids and meet them where they are in order to guide them forward. Many of my girlfriends who are parents have often struggled when their daughters go through puberty and adolescence; the daughters shut down and it becomes impossible for their mothers to reach them. Sometimes, we might need a third party who is more neutral to find the best way to communicate with the children. That phase, when a child is becoming an adult and discovering their independence, a sense of self, and where they belong, is a very difficult time for parents to navigate. They are losing control, and so often the way parents try to gain control is by asserting themselves, setting rules, punishing questionable behavior, and cutting off deeper communication.

As much as we need to educate our children, we need to educate the parents on how to cope with unknown territory. I've seen it over and over again with friends' children during adolescence—they have problems with food, drugs, or grades; they choose the wrong friends or shut down completely. I didn't encounter these particular problems during my own teenage years because I was always so very close to my mother, and we talked about everything. What made those years hard for me was that I was having so many feelings I could not find the words to express, and that created a sense of isolation, loneliness, and lack of trust and safety. What we can do to help our children at that difficult age is to restore their trust and sensitivity, and help them awaken to who they are on a soul level and see themselves as spiritual beings.

The Prayer

Dear Beloved,

My son or daughter is going through the change from being a child to becoming an adult, and it's been hard for me to reach and communicate with them.

They are demonstrating rebellious behavior and it feels like they are turning against me. They are spending hours on social media, talking to their friends, and getting distracted by things that don't serve them. They disconnect from the family and isolate themselves, and I'm at a loss about how to reach them.

My heart is aching for them and for me. I am afraid that they will lose their way, and my hopes and dreams for them are evaporating. I love my child so much and to experience the loss of my relationship with them is very painful for me.

Please guide me to act or not to act. What to say or not to say. Give me patience and understanding so I will find people who can support me. Help me not lose my temper and revert to punishment or get into arguments with them that lead nowhere.

Now I quiet myself, and I ask for the presence. I ask that I may bring forward my child's highest self—their soul—to ask for their support so that I know they have God within, that their spirit is working with them and will help them through their growth.

I ask that I may pull myself back and come to my own center and trust that they have a unique path and all the tools they need to work through the challenges of their lives. I am wholeheartedly here to support the being that they can become, and all I want for them is to become themselves.

Right now I am attached to the way I think things are supposed to be. Please help me bring more light to the situation so that I may find my own wisdom and awaken more deeply into who my child is.

Please protect my child. All I want to know is that they are safe and that they may awaken into the truth of who they are—their heart and purpose and wisdom.

I ask that I trust this is a phase, and he or she will, in perfect time, see the truth and rise to his or her potential.

Please help me be at peace with this situation and find my peace throughout it.

So be it.

43

Partnering with Spirit to Care for Aging Parents

It was such a blessing to be present at both of my parents' passings. My father was in Athens, Greece, when he got very sick with various ailments and was largely confined to his apartment with a caretaker. I was living in New York, and he was always on my mind. I would call him practically every day. I prayed for him, and I had friends praying for him as well. Because he had diabetes, he had only partial eyesight and was not able to read or watch the news. He felt terribly isolated. I carried a lot of the suffering that he was going through and felt inadequate for not being able to help him. My only comfort was that I often went to visit him in Greece, and prayed and stood by his side, which gave him and me tremendous relief.

Similarly, my mother, who was living with my sister in Los Angeles when she became sick, had many difficult months with congestive heart failure. She was stronger and more resilient than my father, so she wouldn't always call for help and didn't like being dependent on anyone. My father was much more open about asking for affection, love, and care, which always pulled on my heartstrings.

Watching one's parents age, become weak, and suffer from illness can be unbearably hard. We are forced to become the parents of our parents, and the child in us cries out. On one hand we hurt, and on the other hand we must make decisions for them, hold strong, and be the caretaker. Whether we are close to them or far away, they are always with us. Praying daily for them, for ourselves, and for acceptance of the transitions of life is so important. We must bring in the divine presence and the higher consciousness in this process of letting go that, ultimately, we all must go through, whether it is with our parents, a loved one, or ourselves. It's a big part of life that no one really prepares us for.

I was there when my father passed away, and I witnessed his readiness to go. I remember it so vividly. I was lying next to him as my father kept saying to me in Greek, "You have always been my comfort," which was true. I was always there for him—to love him, support him, and bring him joy by making him feel part of our lives from afar. As I lay next to him, I heard the sweet voice of spirit almost whisper to me, "It is done." A presence came in at that moment, like a canopy of love that moved me from my place beside him and walked me through his apartment, gathering a few of his belongings that he treasured. I left his home and went to my hotel feeling as if I was escorted by a tremendous peace and love. How incredible it is to bear witness to someone who is ready to leave this realm in peace; in that moment, I could feel myself letting go of my father even though he was still physically with us.

The next morning, my sister arrived from the States to be with him. On our way to see him for what we believed would be the last time, we got a call from his assistant. She told us that he had just died. When we arrived, we went into the bedroom where he lay and sat by his side, crying and praying. His soul presence was palpable. We were aware that, although my father was gone in body, his beautiful, light-filled spirit was present. At that moment, I had this profound awareness about life and death—that life continues in a different form that transcends the physical and is part of the greater mystery of the soul consciousness. It is as if one door closes and another opens, and we enter into another sphere. And there it was. In that moment, my father was bringing home the greatest gift of life: living doesn't end. Life as we know it might end, but if we open our spiritual eye, we will see that there is a spiritual life that is as real as our next breath. For that, I am forever grateful to him, and my love affair with my father has continued in many forms and dreams, and in an awareness that his spirit is very much alive.

So, for any of you who have parents who are ailing in assisted living, or are suffering an illness that impedes communication, it is so important to keep prayer alive in your heart. Hold on to the greater awareness of the spirit connection that bridges this world and the world beyond.

The Prayer

Dear Beloved,

Watching my parent be sick and having to care for them is one of the hardest things I've ever gone through.

As they are preparing to leave this earth, not knowing exactly when it will occur, I ask for the stamina, endurance, and strength of a spiritual warrior to help me go through this phase.

I ask that my emotions, which are pulled between holding on and letting go, settle. I ask that I may have the wisdom to know what is to be done, each day in each decision, to bring to them the greatest light from the highest place so they may know that they're not alone in this challenging time.

I also ask that I may get out of my own way and rise above my personality, my emotions, and the child in me so that I may be a loving presence for my parent on every level, looking after them to the best of my ability and asking for support from other friends or family.

I ask that grace be extended to my parent so that they may know that, in this difficult time, they are loved and protected.

This process of letting go is so excruciating for me. It's like some part of me is being ripped apart. Show me how to have more kindness and tenderness with myself as I go through this with the presence of the divine and God by my side, to not collapse but rise.

I allow myself the expression of every feeling that may arise and as I release it, there is a transformation. I know that I am never alone, even in this.

Thank you, God. Thank you, divine presence. I exhale and I receive the stillness. In the stillness, I surrender to the bigger plan and I trust that there is perfection in the timing of life. My heart is at peace. Let me feel embraced in the physical world and in the spiritual world.

So be it!

44

Finding Comfort and Grace in the Loss of a Loved One

I lost my parents three and a half months apart. My father died May 11, 2000, and my mother died August 23, 2000. It was my first experience losing loved ones and I didn't know if I could survive it.

After my parents passed, I walked around for about a year feeling like I was in a daze, as if I'd had surgery and both my arms had been cut off. As the people we love leave us, there is a huge adjustment, especially with parents, because our souls and DNA are so connected to them. It feels like free-falling, and that feeling of grief takes over one's physical, emotional, and spiritual being. During that time of grieving, I reached out to close friends who cared for me and had known my parents. I was extremely vulnerable and transparent, and I would often tell them, "I'm having a hard day. I could use a hug, a visit, a talk, or a cry." But I still had to walk the path alone, even with all the friends I had around me and the tools I had from my spiritual teachings.

So when people are going through grief or loss, I relate, and there are no words to say to someone—give them love and compassion and a safe space for them to cry. If you can cry a lot, it's wonderful. Let yourself feel the exquisite vulnerability and everything that goes with it—the sadness, the sorrow, the loss, the void. When you are feeling out of control, left out and abandoned, surrender to it. Don't try to suppress, hide, or alter it. Don't go against the tide of grief. Go with it and let it run its course.

The thing I missed the most about my parents was how loved by them I felt. Not only did I love them, but they treasured me and knew me so deeply that when their day-to-day love was gone, I believed it was irreplaceable, and its absence left an emptiness. It wasn't until a year later that I started to integrate their love into my life and fill the emptiness with love, acceptance, and a sense that their presence is always with me. Because my father was so dependent on me, and I used to worry so much about my mother's health, their respective passings freed up a lot of my energy. With them gone, I could put all that energy into my life and my creativity. I started to expand, and I felt their blessing in my creative work, and their love for me continued to infuse my life.

I know now in my heart of hearts that love never dies. Once we love someone, maybe their physical body is gone, maybe they go silent in us for a while, but we always have their love. If you have lost a loved one, prayer can be a bridge for you to access their spirit and find the courage to go on. So let us pray. Please add your own words to honor the person you lost.

The Prayer

Dear Beloved,

I open my heart to you so I can find comfort in the pain of losing my loved one. I wonder how I will be able to go on without the love of this special person. I ask that you may touch where all my tears, sadness, and pain sit.

I feel at a loss as to how to ask for what I need, for I don't know what that is. What I really need is for the person I love to be with me, and it is so hard for me to believe that I can go on without them or accept that they are gone.

I ask for whatever relief, insight, and awareness can be given to help me get through this loss, sadness, and grief with grace. Help me reach out to others that love me and allow their love to heal me. Allow me to know that your love for me is there as well.

For the part of me that is hurting, I ask to give myself permission to release the pain and let my tears flow to their fullest.

In all this, I ask for your grace. I ask for patience and tenderness with myself in this process. I allow the miracle of time to show me that the love we have for each other will never die and that I may feel their presence touch upon me, comfort me, and bring me greater awareness that they are alive in their soul.

I trust that my prayer is heard. In the silence, I lift my heart to be at peace and comforted by you.

So be it.

45

Being at Home Wherever You Are

When I left Greece to study abroad in London, and then later moved on to Los Angeles, I never quite felt at home. It wasn't until I was studying psychology at the University of Santa Monica that I became aware of how a part of me—the part connected to my culture, my family, and my early life—had been interrupted. I had put layers over myself to cover, adapt, and fit in. When I spoke my mother tongue of Greek, I felt a deep, visceral connection to my true self and my joy. But I didn't know how to integrate my true self with the self that I was now becoming in these foreign countries. So, this created a sense of scarcity inside of me: the scarcity of work, money, relationships, love, and connection. When I trace that scarcity back I realize it had to do with feeling displaced. Although I had embraced this country as my home, I had not yet integrated the Greek girl in me.

When I returned to Greece to visit my father for the holidays, that part of me came alive, yet I would never consider living in Greece again. My education and my many years abroad had shaped me and pointed my life in a different direction. Yet, paradoxically, I still didn't feel entirely at home in America. I often meet people who, having moved to a state or country different than the one they grew up in, also experience this feeling of not belonging and missing home. When I lived in New York and often took taxis, I would have many conversations with drivers who were from all over the world—Pakistan, India, Nigeria, Jamaica—people who had come to America seeking opportunity and a better way of life. I could feel their sense of displacement. I have so much compassion for people who are in this country yet constantly miss another place—their family, their home, their country, their land.

Over time, I learned to keep my connection to Greece alive. When I got together with my Greek friends, ate at a Greek restaurant, listened to Greek music, or went home to Greece, the aliveness of that culture was ignited in me. People would ask me, "Do you miss your home?" I replied, "No, because I have found a home in myself and I create experiences that connect me to what I miss."

In truth, practically everyone in America is an immigrant. So finding our connection to the community that we feel we belong to is essential. When I found my spiritual teacher and community, I started to feel more connected to a community in Los Angeles—one beyond my language, ethnicity, and culture—and I was able to bring my Greek spirit wherever I went. Instead of feeling like I didn't belong, I discovered that I belonged just as much as anyone belongs, and I started to create my own extended family. My mother used to say, "Out of all the people we meet, there are a few that become a part of our essential family. They are not our blood family, but we feel a sense of recognition and connection there with people who are like-minded. Then, we all become instruments of an orchestra that play symphonies together." I was very blessed to find that community in my spiritual group. Everyone is very much their own person, but we share a common thread: our hearts are open to one another, and we follow a path of soul awareness.

The question I want to ask you is this: Is there a part of you that feels uprooted? You don't need to be able to pinpoint why you feel that way. Grounding yourself in your life is a process that requires tremendous awareness and openness to receive support and assistance from within and without, so you can set yourself in the right direction. The feeling of displacement feels like a ship without an anchor. You feel like you're going to drift with the wind, the boat keeps rocking, and it can feel very unsettling. In those conditions, it's difficult to create the life you want. What part of you needs to be anchored? Remember, as Hafiz wrote, "The place where you are right now, God circled on a map for you." As you open up to embrace where you are, you can see what opportunities and wisdom are in store for you, and you will start to feel a sense of liberation and peace within yourself.

The Prayer

Dear Beloved,

I open my heart and ask for the light to shine on all levels of my consciousness—physical, emotional, mental, and spiritual—and I open my heart to you.

For so long I have missed a sense of home. I feel disconnected, uprooted, and misplaced.

I go through my life but it's like going through the motions because I don't quite feel connected to myself, seen by people, or accepted as part of a community. I ask that I may change my outlook to see new possibilities, develop a connection to this country where I live, and see all there is for me here.

I keep looking back and thinking there might be another place that I'm supposed to be, where I would feel a greater sense of connection and belonging, but I'm wondering whether that is true or not. I ask for clarity, inspiration, and a miracle to know the spirit lives in me, breathes in me, and works with me wherever I am regardless of land, language, culture, or sense of familiarity.

I miss the warm connection of my language and my country, so show me where and with whom I might find that in this country. Send me experiences that delight me, in which I can feel connected, joyful, and at home, with compatible friends and people I care for and who care for me.

I prepare a way for the spirit to enter and start creating these experiences.

Show me where I can find the resonance with others who are my people. Whether they are from other cultures, speak other languages, or hail from other traditions, may I find my sense of family.

I thank you for opening my eyes and bringing me home to myself. I trust that this inner light can create the magic I am looking for in the world.

So be it!

Prayer for Infertility Struggles

Dear Beloved,

As I realize that I may not be able to bear children, I experience a deep sense of loss and grief, and a feeling that I am denied a woman's right to bear or have children. I am bereft and heartbroken.

I present myself to the light and the wisdom of my soul and ask that I may be assisted in looking at this situation— this condition—as a blessing, and recognize that there may be another avenue for me: I could adopt a child or let go of the idea of being a mother.

I ask that I may not carry this as a burden or punishment in any way, or feel that I am at odds with my body or believe that my body has failed me. I ask that I may come into the greater forgiveness of the greater plan of my soul, and trust that there is a gift to be found hidden in these circumstances.

I ask to be kind and tender and nurturing to myself, have compassion for myself, and most of all, release the pain, grief, and heartache. I ask that I not look upon women who so easily bear children with envy but with compassion, accepting that their destiny is different from mine.

I am so grateful for any assistance I may receive in releasing my sadness and shame, and I ask for the renewal of my life force, my joy, my enthusiasm, and my sense of purpose.

May I have the wisdom to return often to this request, trusting that the spirit will be there for me, even in those moments when I am overwhelmed by the pain and feel I cannot go on. I know that I can always return to you for solace and upliftment and guidance.

I quiet myself and I receive.

So be it.

46

Love Yourself the Way You Want to Be Loved

When someone doesn't love you the way you want them to, that doesn't mean they aren't loving you with all they have. So often we expect the people who are close to us—family, friends, or loved ones—to love us in the way we want to be loved. I have often felt let down when people close to me don't react to me in the way I would like. This comes in many different forms and in all sorts of relationships in our lives—on big occasions, like birthdays and anniversaries, and at times when we have good or bad news to share.

When my parents separated, my mother moved out and my sister and I went to live with her. But I was still very close to my father. I loved him dearly and felt bereaved by the fact we weren't living together anymore. I would call him to talk to him, but he wouldn't come to the phone, and his assistant would tell me that my father was busy or not at work, which I knew wasn't true. When we were together, he was distracted and withdrawn.

It took me years to figure out that my father was deeply wounded from having spent a year and a half in a concentration camp in Germany during the Second World War. Having extramarital relationships was his way of acting out. When my mother decided to leave him and take me and my sister with her, my father was devastated. His ego didn't allow him to be vulnerable with his daughters, to tell us how hard it was for him. Instead, he put up a stoic façade and shut off from my mother. It was many years later that he admitted to me how much he had missed my sister and me, and how hurt he was by my mother's decision, but at the time he didn't know how to express it. As a young girl, I didn't understand what he was going through, and the experience of his withdrawal from our family was extremely painful and disappointing, and I internalized it and felt helpless.

I have had to work diligently on my hypersensitivity, becoming aware of the parts of myself that expect people to act a certain way toward me. Over time, I have learned to take things less personally. How liberating is that? When people do show affection and warmth in intimate, personal relationships, it's absolutely wonderful and heartwarming, but our expectations can run wild. When you go to your workplace and somebody passes you by without saying hello, you may feel ignored and insecure—you might think: why don't they like me? Their actions might have nothing to do with you! They might just be extremely preoccupied or focused. Someone may abruptly ask you to do something without considering what else you're working on, and in that moment, you might feel like you're being walked all over. But we are responsible for our own reactions. This is where our maturity and understanding comes in, so we aren't ruled by our expectations, constantly feeling disappointed when others fail to meet them.

We cannot give people a script of what we want them to do or say. We can't say, "This is how I want you to respond, this is how I want you to reach out, this is how I like to be interacted with." If we have an open relationship with someone, we can explain to them how we would like to be treated, but by no means can we put the burden on someone else to meet our expectations without knowing them. We must look at that part of ourselves that is reacting to others and see where we are giving our power away. We all long to be seen and loved as we are, and when people don't react to us the way we'd like them to, we can start to feel we don't matter and are being discounted. So what do we do? What decisions do we make? It's very empowering when we take responsibility for seeing and loving ourselves as we are and demand less of other people.

In intimate relationships, it's important to express how you would like to be loved and communicated with. A friend of mine had to teach her husband how to talk to her so she wouldn't feel bullied. Around friends, he would often say such things as "Go get me this" or "Do that." She started to put these alternative phrases together and taught him how to ask her in a way that engaged her and made her want to do those things for him. In personal relationships, we can educate people and guide them to the way we want to be treated, but this requires us to be vulnerable with those people with whom we have intimate relationships. However, you can't have the same openness with coworkers, clients, acquaintances, or social friends. You can only open this line of communication with those people who you value and who are very close to you.

If we haven't connected to that part of ourselves that wants to be loved, we often operate from scarcity, lack, and the assumption that others should love us the way we expect them to love us. Obviously, we all crave affection and attention, and it's wonderful receiving it the way we want. But could it be that the way people are treating us is a reflection of the way we are treating ourselves, and they're just mirroring the way we address ourselves? For example, if somebody was cold with me, I would ask myself if I've been cold with myself. If someone doesn't reach out to connect with me, I would ask if I've connected with myself. If someone doesn't appreciate me, I would ask if I've been appreciating myself. We have the power to take full responsibility for our own care. If we notice where the gaps are within ourselves, we may notice that our fullness runneth over, and we are so filled with our own love that the external world starts to reflect how we are with ourselves.

So, the prayer I'd like to share is helpful in reversing the paradigm and filling ourselves to capacity. Then, when others don't love us or act the way we'd like them to, we are okay with it.

The Prayer

Dear Beloved,

I ask for the spirit to fill me, protect me, and surround me. I ask that I may open my heart to the fullness of myself, to be more receptive to hear my inner guidance.

I bring now, into the light, any areas in myself that I have abandoned, neglected, or ignored.

I now ask that any parts of me that feel disconnected, unloved, or separated from myself be bridged by delighting in my own being and my own self. In those areas in which I feel lacking, insecure, or unfulfilled, I ask to not look to others to fulfill them but instead open up a dialogue with myself to know what the deeper parts of me need and how I can meet those needs.

When I reach out to others to ask for what I want or need, I ask to do it from a place of freedom, honoring myself by knowing that I have the right to ask for what I want. I ask to be okay when others don't give me what I need.

I look with the eyes of love and understanding, knowing that others, too, have their own process, and how they are, or are not, with me has nothing to do with me but is more about their own process and themselves.

I now release into the light my expectations of how others should be with me, and I go free. I fill myself with the joy of myself and the deepest acceptance of my relationships with others—just how they are.

I am grateful for who I am and for my willingness to bring the spirit into my life.

So be it!

47

You Are the One
You're Looking For

Some people can create wonderful, happy relationships easily and effortlessly. They meet when they're young and a few years later they live together, get married, have a family, and live happily ever after. Then there are the rest of us: people who deeply struggle with dating, longing to find somebody but it doesn't work out. This is a prayer for those people yearning for their life partner.

Before you pray, it's important to be very clear about what you want (or don't want), why you want it (or don't want it), and the beliefs you have around love. When I was young, I saw that my mother was unhappy with my father because he wasn't faithful to her, and that memory of not feeling safe with a man, and the belief that I couldn't necessarily trust myself to find the right person, was embedded in me from a very young age. Later in life, as the relationships I created failed to make me happy and I kept attracting men who were not emotionally available, I didn't know what to do to make something different happen.

I had to do a lot of inner work to realize that my mother's beliefs had been transferred to me. As much as I wanted a relationship with a man, what I really wanted in life was to express myself fully. I was unsure that I could be true to myself while in an intimate relationship. My pattern had always been to merge with a man and take care of him, prioritizing him over myself. When I really considered what I wanted, I realized that being by myself was ultimately a choice I could make to serve my soul's expression and experience my highest good.

One year, my spiritual teacher and I were celebrating my birthday and I said to him, "Here I am, another year, still single." He replied, "You're not single; you are singular." That forever removed the stigma of being single for me. My advice to younger women who are struggling to find love and fulfilling relationships is to always aim for your own self-healing and a commitment to yourself first. Trust, as you grow, that you will find the person who is yours to find. If we're coming from a place of neediness and lack, the other person is going to sense it, and nine times out of ten, the universe is going to bring people to us that activate those places in which we don't feel whole so that we can address them. As you are looking for your ideal life partner, keep in mind that relationships are the perfect way to work out our own issues, and most of all, they teach us how to give and receive love. Any insecurities, judgments, agendas, and patterns that we have will be revealed in an intimate relationship. The more unconditionally loving and accepting we are with ourselves, the more we'll be able to authentically show up in a relationship.

When I was living alone in New York, I was in love with a man, and I expected him to be my romantic ideal of a partner. I would soon discover that he was completely different from the image I was projecting onto him. In truth, I didn't really know who he was. When the glow disappeared, and I started to see clearly, I was crushed because I never took the time to truly know him. He was a wonderful and attractive man in many ways, but he was wounded from his previous relationships, starting with his mother. The more intimate we became, the more he withdrew, which was extremely painful for me.

I remember calling my mother and telling her I thought he was "the one" because I so longed to find "the one." My mother, who also wanted me to find "the one," told me to just keep enjoying myself and I would know in time. What I now know for sure is that there is no such thing as "the one." What's important is that you are loving, growing, and enjoying life with the one you are with right now. The more present we become with them and ourselves, the more clearly our hearts will reveal to us whether this is a long-term relationship: a partner for life or someone we are just having fun with for now.

If we want to create an ideal relationship with all the criteria that matter to us, it's important that we design it with spirit as our partner, allowing our souls to reveal to us more of who we are and more of who an ideal partner would be for us. We can approach this in a higher and more soulful way, and trust in our divine plan. I heard one of the greatest prayers when a friend of mine prayed to God, saying, "Please, God, bring me my perfect match." He said to me, "You know, I don't really know who my perfect match is—I have my ideas—but I think I'm going to hand it over to my higher self and my spirit so I can see what they have for me." Indeed, after a few months of declaring his prayers, he met a woman who was fifteen years older than him—who he never would've thought would be a good match for him on paper. As it turns out, they had a very fulfilling relationship for many years until it was over. They never got married, but he said it was one of the best things that has happened in his life. I love that prayer, and I love keeping an open heart and mind to see what shows up.

So let us pray that the elements and qualities we seek in a

perfect match come alive in us, so that we will feel whole and complete within ourselves.

The Prayer

Dear Beloved,

I open my heart, center myself, and quiet my mind.

I feel ready and open to have the perfect partner in my life.

I am also timid and scared to move on with something that could so change my life as it is.

I have fears of being hurt, choosing the wrong person, facing rejection, or feeling captive and confined, so I ask for guidance on what steps I need to take to open myself up and trust that the right person is out there for me. Then I can also be that special person for someone who's looking for a partner like me.

I ask for the perfect plan for my life to be revealed to me, as I see this experience of loving someone and being loved by someone become a reality.

I ask for strength in myself to release the fear that there is no one out there for me, to embrace my vulnerability and the openness of my heart, and to strengthen my deepest desires so that I can gently reveal them to myself and let my heart receive the one that is for me.

May I be patient, compassionate, and loving with myself as I live in anticipation of the joy that is to come. I keep the fire lit within me, not out of a sense of lack, but because I sense a garden whose gate I have yet to open.

Most of all, help me know that I deserve to have this partner—that I deserve to be loved exactly how I am and to have the love, partnership, and togetherness that I so long for.

So be it!

VI

Transforming

48

Embracing All Aspects of the Feminine in You

When I was writing a book about the Greek goddesses, it was a revelation to me to learn that all the qualities of the goddesses are embedded in us as part of our feminine nature—from Athena's wisdom and compassion to Artemis's focus and sense of independence; from Demeter's qualities of nurturing and abundance to Hera's power and gift of partnerships and Hestia's sense of the sacred. But none embodies femininity more than Aphrodite; she is the goddess of sensuality, romance, and feminine power. In each archetype, I discovered qualities that were part of me but might have been suppressed or denied. I was brought up in a culture in which women were the caretakers and nurturers, and the dynamic between men and women was not equal. Having a very sensual nature myself, I had to release judgments and shame about my sexuality. I needed to embrace the spirit of independence through the goddess Artemis— staying focused, following the principles of clear direction and autonomy. I had exiled those parts of myself because I felt that it was not feminine to be direct, to be clear, or to have so many boundaries. I judged it in others, and I judged it in myself. I saw it as unfeminine because it wasn't sweet or sensual.

And yet, it is a great mighty quality in all of us women. In fact, I see so many women who embody Artemis's archetype— direct and clear—while their kindness and compassion is hidden underneath the surface. If that resonates with you, I encourage you to embrace those qualities as well. You may have become extremely direct and driven in your career, but at the expense of the feminine nature that is playful, joyful, and sensual. Each one of us must find our balance and wholeness in the feminine, especially in a culture that discourages the full expression of femininity. As I have stepped into different roles in my life—as an author, a speaker, a performer, a producer, a nurturing human being, and more—I have embraced qualities from each of the goddesses to move forward into the fullness of my expression instead of relying on the outside world to give me permission to express the various aspects of myself. For me, this is the true embodiment of embracing the feminine within me. In truth, it was goddess in action. When fear would arise— *How would I raise the money? Who would come to see the show? Would I fail?*—all these human emotions threatened to overwhelm me. I had to bring my bow and arrow like Artemis, my sword and shield like Athena, and move forward like a warrior goddess.

If you need to move your hips, your belly, your arms and shoulders, flip your hair and dance like a wild woman to free yourself up, just do it! Maybe you need to have an experience in which you let yourself go—maybe you need to make love—and that's okay. If you need the experience of saying clearly what you need to say, to voice your opinions and your thoughts and say no one hundred times before you know you have the right to say no, just do it and practice it even if it feels awkward and uncomfortable. If you need to learn how to love more and be more generous, kind, and compassionate, focus on an area of your life and practice the muscle that is the loving in you, that is the compassionate woman in you, because that needs to be awakened in every woman for the good of our humanity. If you need to ask other women to help you get out of relationships that don't work for you, then ask for that. But I want you to know that you have every right to stand on this earth in the power and uniqueness of who you are, and not look left and right for approval. When you tap into the resilient spirit of the goddesses—find it in yourself, plant yourself in it, and embody it—no one can take it away from you. But we can only learn this through taking action and moving forward; it's not something we learn from books or movies. Silent prayer can help us conjure this feminine power in ourselves and cultivate it in our external lives, wherever we are.

All experiences of womanhood should be honored because they are sacred. This awareness will also help men awaken to their feminine and masculine sides, and they, too, will be released from the male archetype of rage, fear, and anger, while hiding the vulnerable and tender parts of themselves. This stereotypical male archetype has made them believe that, in order to be a leader, they have to disconnect from their emotional heart. All those limiting beliefs have held men hostage for so long. When women step into the fullness of themselves, we allow men to also step into their power from a more connected place. We are all evolving together, and we women must usher in this awakening, take a stand and claim our power and wisdom, just as the goddesses showed us.

Isn't it wonderful to know that we, as women, have this ability to move within these aspects of ourselves? We are not made from one note; instead we are made from many notes that, strung together, create the symphony of our being. Any color we see in others, we have in ourselves. My prayer for every woman is to feel her wholeness in her human divine self and not deny any of these aspects of herself. If you are lacking one or the other, you can pray for those qualities that you need for your wholeness to be present and awaken within you.

The Prayer

Dear Beloved,

As I walk on this earth in my female form, I am grateful for being embodied as a woman. But many limitations and projected beliefs have also limited my feminine, divine expression.

For a long time, I was thought of as a little girl that needed to be saved. So often, I wanted to act out, express myself—my voice and my will—and do what I wanted. I would encounter this wall, forbidding me from moving forward in the fullness of my expression.

So much of my attention and my life seemed to depend on men—how they made me feel, how they loved me, how they gave me permission to live my life—and my power was always diminished and crushed. I stayed behind the scenes, unseen and unfulfilled.

Then one day, I met the feminine archetypes that were

powerful, complete within themselves, independent, wise, fearless, confident, and full of gusto and presence.

Now, in this altar of the goddess, this feminine archetype charged with spiritual energy, love, and divine guidance, I ask that I release those parts of me that feel small, not enough, helpless, and dependent on men for survival. I bless them and release them with no judgments and no fear.

I ask that the feminine power of these qualities may infuse my body, my heart, my being, and the very core of my very self, that I may open my arms, extend all the way, and embrace these qualities of wisdom, compassion, focus, independence, vision, sensuality, joy and mirth, grace and wonderment, transformation and fearless expression. May all these qualities now light up in me and light the path before me, so that I may see beyond my limited, conditioned self and awaken in my radiant feminine spirit form that is whole, complete, and filled with the divine light.

May the little girl in me dare to stand up and have the courage to own this power of mine. I am declaring it as mine. I claim it as mine. I breathe it in, and I begin to embody it day by day.

Most of all, I am at peace knowing that womanhood is complete within me. There is no death, only glorious rebirth. In this new vision of my feminine, I am now reborn. I kneel in front of the altar and give thanks, for now I know the truth of who I am.

So be it!

49

How to Navigate Being an Empath

It wasn't until later in my life that I became aware I was an *empath,* a Greek word derived from the root *pathos,* meaning suffering, and *en,* meaning in or with. An empath is a person with the ability to understand the mental or emotional state of another individual and to put oneself in another's position. I definitely identify as an empath. My empathetic nature originated in my childhood, especially around my father, who had endured a lot of trauma and turmoil in his life. I could feel the depths of his pain and suffering. Throughout my childhood, I felt an incredible sense of responsibility to alleviate some of this pain and suffering in order to restore some balance to his life. I did everything I could to bring him joy and happiness and make him feel better. He was always in my thoughts, and I sensed his heavy heart. It wasn't until he died that I was able to break my attachment to him and become more aware of how that pattern had woven itself into many other relationships in my life.

Throughout my life, I often attracted people who had problems or difficulties and needed help. Somehow, I seemed to gravitate to them, and I became a lot of people's confidante. Men would tell me about their problems with women, women would tell me about their problems with men, and on and on. If I went to a gathering, social or professional, it never failed that I would connect with someone who had an issue that needed to be heard. For some reason, I had cast myself as the caretaker, people fixer, and on-call therapist without being paid!

Through a lot of inner work, I realized how "other" oriented I was. I was always managing and taking care of other people, and their well-being was extremely interconnected with my own. Could I make them feel better? Could I find solutions for them? Could I step in and fix it all for them? Those concerns especially intensified around my family. I started to ask where others began and ended, and where I began and ended. The boundaries had been blurred. It took me years to rewire myself not to be completely immersed in others' journeys and to allow them the dignity of their lessons and challenges. My greatest realization was that the pattern of taking care of others was my own resistance to fully taking care of myself. I hoped if I took good care of others, they would in turn take care of me. Underneath it all was a deep longing for intimacy, connection, and love.

As I became more self-aware, I was able to distinguish between what was mine and what was theirs and relieve myself of feeling responsible for other people's emotional states or challenges. It was liberating to discover that taking on other people's problems doesn't serve anyone. As empaths, we believe that by feeling other people's pain, hurt, or discomfort, we will make them feel better, but in fact, this doesn't make them feel better, and the detriment of it is that they still have their pain and now so do we. I had to tap into my wisdom and become more detached, putting some distance, with love, between them and me, trusting that they, too, have a higher self and God in them. I can be there for them with compassion and listen with a full heart so they can awaken to their own wisdom and solutions. There is a tremendous power in holding the presence of love and letting the light in us touch the light in another.

Being an empath is not an easy pattern to change because I believe it is mapped onto our DNA. It's a wonderful thing to care for others, but if we sacrifice taking care of ourselves in the process, we must shed light on that pattern and ask for inner wisdom to navigate it within ourselves. Let us pray together, to shift the pattern and maintain a loving and caring heart while accessing wiser choices for ourselves and others.

The Prayer

Dear Beloved,

I now ask for the light of the spirit to protect, surround, and embrace me.

I bring into the light the pattern of feeling overly responsible for others and concerned with their well-being. I end up losing my own center, overextending myself to others, and absorbing their emotional pain and discomfort.

I now ask that I be given the wisdom to take care of myself, to develop a deeper relationship with the beloved in me, and to ruthlessly address my own needs, no matter how small they are. I also ask that the intimacy and sweetness I long to have with others may start first between myself and God so that I come to others in the fullness of myself.

I ask that I may become discerning of what is mine to do and what is to be given over to the higher energy of God and light, so I may relinquish my need to always be there for others. Help me release the attachment to taking care of others in order to feel my worth, value, and purpose.

Allow me to experience the freedom of knowing that each person has their own journey and their own path, and let me be a source of love and support as I help others remember their own light and their own soul power.

I now allow that pattern to be transformed in me, and trust and affirm that I am valued and worthy as I am, anchored in my own God-given loving heart and my trust that all is well.

I trust the processes that others have in their lives. Help me open my spiritual eye so I may see through the higher perspective of spirit and be free.

So be it.

Prayer to Bring Light to Those Who Are Suffering

Dear Beloved,

There is so much atrocity in the world around me and so much I cannot understand. I feel helpless and unable to alleviate the suffering, and I feel the heaviness from those who are isolated, who have been inflicted upon, and who have survived great trauma and adversity.

Although I alone can do nothing, I ask that the light of peace and understanding, which is of the higher wisdom, be showered upon them so that they may be comforted. I ask that they be shown a way to live on this earth and still have their light. May the grace of the spirit touch upon them now in their conditions.

I also ask that I may find my peace as I look at those who suffer and at all the injustices in the world. I ask that I may be a bearer of peace and light for all those in need.

So be it.

50

Living with a Sense of Timelessness

To see a World in a Grain of Sand,
And a Heaven in a Wild Flower,
Hold Infinity in the palm of your hand
And Eternity in an hour

—WILLIAM BLAKE

One of the reasons I love performing is that time stops. Ever since I was a young girl in drama school, when I was on stage acting a part, I felt so fully present and alive. There is no other thought on my mind when I am acting, performing, or speaking, because it requires me to be so present. It is the most exhilarating feeling. A few days before my one-woman show, *Conversations with the Goddesses,* a dear friend of mine who teaches a wonderful breathing technique, came to offer her support and give me a session. While I was lying on the table, breathing and intoning in a relaxed way, she said these magic words: "Darling, let yourself be breathed." At that moment, I realized the incredible power of the breath of life through me. If you think about it for a moment, we don't *do* anything to take a breath; it is freely given to us. It is the miracle of life in us.

When I arrived at the venue on the day of the performance, with two hundred people in attendance in a beautiful garden and full camera crew ready to film the show, I was riding on the wave of my breath, which felt full of grace and beyond the constriction of time. I started to perform, moving from one monologue to the next in a completely relaxed flow. I was utterly present with the audience, not missing a beat. I felt as if I was completely out of my own way, letting spirit take the lead while I was fully enjoying the experience. It was seamless. Everybody felt it—the director, the camera crew, the audience—they were all part of the experience. When we finished later in the evening, I don't think I had ever felt such a sense of presence and bliss. I was ecstatic. I use the memory of that experience as a reference for myself, to remind me that when I go beyond my thoughts and emotions and allow the power of the spirit to breathe through me, time doesn't really exist and I feel as though I have transcended its limitations.

During the coronavirus pandemic, I experienced two different feelings in reference to the concept of time. Staying at home, I experienced how quickly the day moved from one thing to the next, but at the same time, we didn't know when this period would end or how we would come out of it. So, there was this paradox of the speed and slowness of time. On the one hand, the days and months seemed to fly by—how rapidly it became spring and then summer and then Christmas and New Year's, and then we were headed into another spring, still constricted by the pandemic. On the other hand, it seemed as though the pandemic would last forever. More than at any other time in my life, I realized the only way to conquer the impatience and the frustration of time going too fast or too slow was to be completely present, like I was when performing the *Conversations with the Goddesses,* but this time without an audience or a script. Can I be present while I'm making my coffee, or eating, or thinking about this book that I'm writing? While I'm on a Zoom call, or walking, or looking over my bank statement, or organizing my drawers? This is a prayer for giving ourselves the greatest gift of being fully present no matter what we're doing or what's going on around us. Can we let go of our judgments, worries, preoccupations, and anticipations of the future and instead move into the higher altitude of the breath, the spirit in us?

The Prayer

Dear Beloved,

I feel the pressure and the panic of time going by. I feel that I don't even have time to have a moment with you.

Inside my head, I hear these words all the time: I don't have enough time. There is no time. Where did the time go?

My heart longs to experience a sense of timelessness, to be above time, to know that in the constraints of my mind and the physical world, I can still attune to the universal clock that has a rhythm, a pace, like the river of life that flows and knows its direction.

I ask now that I may open my mind to know the timelessness of my existence. In the midst of my doings, my actions, my to-do lists, and all the demands of my life— I ask that I move into the rhythm that the universe has so brilliantly and intelligently constructed. Just as the planets turn on their axes in their own time, may I become connected to the divine timing of my life.

Like my cells that have their own life force, in constant motion yet never hectic, I ask that I, too, tap into the source of knowing that as I slow down, I will move into the perfect pace of my life, letting go of the pressure, the overwhelming feelings that deplete me, and the uncertainty.

I ask that the peace that reigns over all things be reinstated in me right now. I call it forward, and I allow it to supersede my thoughts and emotions and overtake me, as I become more of an observer and less of a worrier.

I am grateful for allowing this in my life. I am grateful to know that there is another way. I ask that day by day I am redirected to move into the natural flow of my spirit. Thank you.

So be it!

51

Forgiveness: The Greatest Gift of All

Many years after my parents had separated, when my sister and I were grown and living in Los Angeles with my mother, my father came to visit us and his granddaughters. It was toward the end of his life, and he was suffering from many health problems, so we helped him find medical care in California. After a few months of being with us, it was time for him to go back to Greece, and we all knew that he would likely never return to California.

The final day had come. His bags were packed and the car waited in the driveway to take him to the airport. He hugged each one of us and said his goodbyes. My sister, my mother, and

I walked him to the car. Just before he got into the car, he turned and reached for my mother's hands. He looked at her for what he knew would be the last time and began to weep, and he said to my mother: *Forgive me, my Elli. Forgive me, Elli-moo.* It was one of the most powerful moments in my life, witnessing my frail father as he let go of the pain he had caused my mother over the years.

My mother stood there, silent, allowing him the gift of asking for forgiveness; it was clear that she was moved to the core of her being. The pain was melting away, and the love between them was returning. What a sacred moment—what a gift—my father was giving to both of them, asking for forgiveness not just from my mother but from himself, as well, so that he would not carry that pain to his death.

My sister and I stood by, in awe of what we were witnessing. The tenderness was so palpable that I felt the very stones of the house could melt. We kissed our father once again, I promised him that I would visit him soon in Greece, and we watched him drive away. As we walked my mother back into the house, I looked at her, and she seemed radiant and peaceful, as if the hand of love had touched her face.

I realized, at that moment, how powerful the gift of forgiveness can be, not just for the forgiven but for the forgiver. Love releases our body from the harsh and tight restrictions we place upon ourselves when we judge ourselves for our actions. Love pours out from our souls, flowing into our very own cells. Forgiveness releases withheld love, love we have been keeping from others and from ourselves. If we want to feel more love in our lives, forgiveness is the surest way.

Forgiveness doesn't only apply to the big things—the hurts and betrayals. It applies to all sorts of little things that happen throughout the day: losing our temper, messing up a conversation, running late, forgetting an appointment, being left out of a meeting or a gathering—countless situations that arise every day for which we have to forgive both others and ourselves.

Practice forgiveness daily. Forgive yourself for what you do or don't do, for things that happen that you don't like and for things that you want that haven't happened yet. Forgive yourself for all the judgments you make of others, assuming that you know what they are going through when they don't act the way you want them to act. Forgive the judgments you've made of your own life, for your unmet expectations. Then extend this grace and graciousness to the people in your life, to everyone you meet. Do this over and over again because a loving spirit needs constant nurturing and devotion.

The Prayer

Dear Beloved,

I want to move forward.

The past events that disturbed me are still in my thoughts and sitting in my belly, circulating in my consciousness. I want to let go of what happened with this person, but I can't seem to move forward. It's like a rope, pulling me into the deep water, but I want to be at the shore, clear and free.

I now ask that I may move into the presence and bring the presence to the parts of me that hurt and are ruminating in the old.

I ask that I bring forgiveness to judgments of the person and judgments of myself for my inability to control this person or the situation. I ask that I forgive myself for being triggered and have compassion for myself as I let go and accept that this person is who they are and I cannot change them in any way.

Let my ego be set aside so that my spiritual strength may come forward, so I do not need to make myself wrong or make the other person wrong. Let me find the neutral balance and extend the ray of loving to myself and to them—

the ray of loving I know in my heart, the ray of peace, the ray of the uplifting spirit that exists to make all things fall into place.

If there is any other wisdom that may be added here, I will allow it to enter into my heart's ear so that I may hear the subtle guidance instead of the noise of my hurt, my opinions, my thoughts, and my limitations.

Now I expand. I give myself permission to be free and let go of the resonance of the disagreement. I extend kindness to myself and give myself grace. I wipe the slate clean. I forgive and I forget.

So be it.

52

Gratitude: The Key to Happiness and Fulfillment

*Just as the hand, held before the eye, can hide the tallest mountain,
so the routine of everyday life can keep us from seeing the vast
radiance and the secret wonders that fill the world.*
—HASIDIC SAYING, EIGHTEENTH CENTURY

Some time ago, I was taking a flight back to New York after a speaking engagement in Montana. There was an unexpected snowstorm, so the pilot informed us that we would be landing in Salt Lake City late in the evening and staying there overnight. When we reached Salt Lake City, I was sitting at the gate looking for a hotel where I could spend the night once I rebooked my flight. I was in a foul mood, bitching and complaining to myself over the discomfort of this experience when I heard my inner voice say, "Agapi! Get back to your gratitude. The flight landed safely; you have people who love you that you can reach out to; you have a working credit card." As these thoughts came to me, my heart opened up, and I was filled with gratitude that the situation was not worse.

At that exact moment, a dear friend of mine who I kept in close touch with called me to find out how my speech had gone. When I answered, he said, "Where are you? I'm thinking of you." I told him, "I'm in Salt Lake City, stuck with a delayed flight." He said, "That's so funny, I'm coming to Salt Lake City for a seminar, and I have a two-bedroom suite that you could go to, and shower in, and then when I arrive you can stay in the other room, and I'll drive you to the airport in the morning." What is the likelihood of that happening? I had shifted into gratitude without expecting anything in return, and then the unexpected and miraculous happened.

As I've mentioned, I have been writing this book in the middle of the coronavirus pandemic, and so many things we love have been taken away from us. I've started to make a practice of my gratitude for the ordinary little things that are so easy to take for granted. At our home, we have jugs of filtered water delivered, and every time I get a glass of water, I think of a Pakistani man from a story I once read. Every morning he would walk for a few hours to dig a well and draw water to bring to his family. Often the water wasn't clean. Thinking of this man and his tremendous effort is so humbling and prompts me to make a practice of relishing every glass of water I drink.

As the beautiful Hasidic saying at the beginning of this chapter tells us, it is so easy to get caught in the routines of our lives and all that they involve; we can miss the wonders and the majesty of the world. I see the majestic trees in my neighborhood and wonder at their beauty and longevity. I feel the sun-rays and the magic of the wind, and I see the birds flying and cars passing by. Every little thing that is so easy to take for granted becomes a reminder that there is life and beauty. When I stop and take in the wonder around me, I am shifted into gratitude for the miracle of life.

Having Internet, the miraculous FaceTime on iPhones that bring us together in seconds, a curbside cappuccino at my favorite coffee shop, watching *Emily in Paris* with my family and being transported to the magic of the French culture, croissants and all! People I love who I can call and who can call me. Writing this book, which reminds me daily of the power of prayer to shift my mindset. I must shake myself every day not to focus on what I'm missing but to focus on all that I have. Hearing my sister in the next room on endless Zoom calls, running her company, I feel grateful that I am able to be so close to her and my nieces. It is a once-in-a-lifetime opportunity. It opens me to the perspective of using this opportunity to go deeper into the wonder of my life, look at every day with fresh eyes, and bring more God into each moment. Every minute, we can bring the spirit into our lives through gratitude.

Let's do a prayer for those times when you feel stuck, and things are not going as you expected, so the spirit of gratitude, opportunity, and optimism can enter you, and you can transform something that looks dark and gloomy into a sunny and uplifting miracle.

The Prayer

Dear Beloved,

I call forward the light of the spirit to fill me, surround me, and protect me.

I am asking for assistance to shift the sense of anxiety and uncertainty I have about the present circumstances and the future. I ask that I may be able to shift into a sense of peace, trust, and inner connection.

I decide to take myself for a walk in the street and feel the rays of the sun. My heart is filled with all the beauty I'm looking at—the trees that have been here longer than I have and will remain longer than I will.

I'm looking at everything that grows, including me, my family, the people around me, and I am filled with awe.

As the sun beams down on me, warming my body and my heart, I have the deepest, silent reverence for being a recipient of this generosity of life. The very fact that I am moving now, that I'm alive, that I speak, see, and hear, means all of me is immersed in the breath of life.

All I can think and say is, "How did I get so fortunate, so blessed, so lucky?"

So now, I become a heart of gratitude and gratefulness, silently thanking every blade of grass for existing.

I let every cell of mine be transformed and filled with the chorus of millions of voices singing, "Thank you! Thank you!" Thank you to the one that I cannot possibly even begin to know with the limited perception of my mind.

Now I offer back this grateful heart of mine, which is open, with a smile inhabited by a joyful spirit, and I ask that I may be a conduit and a reminder to others of the glory that is life.

So be it.

*If the only prayer you ever say
in your entire life is thank you,
it will be enough.*
—MEISTER ECKHART

Ending Questions

What's the difference between meditation and prayer?
Prayer is an interactive and living process through which we engage the human and divine parts of ourselves in listening and receiving, whereas in meditation we go into a quiet place that allows the mind to rest and reset. Depending on how you practice prayer or meditation, the ritual can look very similar, so the difference may lie in the intention behind each practice.

How do I pray when I feel so alone, upset, and disturbed, and I don't feel I have it in me to pray?
Prayer brings us back to the power of choice. One choice we always have is to start exactly from where we are. If you are alone,

upset, and disturbed, you can use prayer to admit this to your-self and accept the way you are feeling. You can become willing to offer it to the spirit, and this simple yielding opens you to receiving the shift that prayer can bring.

What is the best way to pray for others or have others pray for me?

The best way to pray for others or have others pray for you is to bring the love and caring you hold in your heart for the other person to your practice of prayer and vice versa. You don't need to stand in ceremony; when you are present with your heart, prayer for another becomes effortless, and the words will flow freely.

Is it okay if my prayers are very simple or monosyllabic?

Absolutely! The power of prayer is in its intent. All that mat-ters is how willing you are to receive the inner wisdom that will be offered to you no matter how simple your prayer. In matters of spirituality, we can learn a lot from children and how natural they are when they pray to God. They don't re-hearse their prayers or think too much about how they will sound; they just speak their hearts and minds, and you can do the same.

Is there a best time of day to pray?

The best time to pray is now and now and now. Prayer is available to you anytime, anywhere, in any moment, and one of the greatest gifts of prayer is the knowledge that your connection with the spirit is *always* available to you, like your breath. I like to pray first thing in the morning as I open my eyes. I put my hands together and pause for a moment of inner connection, sending positive energy and light into the day ahead of me.

Should I say my prayers out loud?

I love to say my prayers aloud, however short or long they may be. There is a healing power that comes through the sounds of our voices. My voice connects me to myself, and I feel empowered and centered when I hear myself speak.

Can I pray while I'm driving?

Yes, as long as you don't close your eyes! Practice saying a short little prayer for protection and safety as you start driving and send the light ahead into your journey and recenter yourself.

How do I pray if I don't even believe there is anyone listening and I feel silly?

Always remember that there is a life force in you that is made up of thirty-seven trillion cells that keep you alive every day. You have a body that functions in a miraculous way every single day. You don't have to go anywhere but within yourself to that intelligent life force that knows how to keep you alive. If you don't believe there is anyone listening, pray to that life force inside of you, which isn't silly at all. That life force deserves your reverence, communion, and gratitude.

There's a phrase in the Bible that says *pray insistently*. Can you tell me what that means?

If we make prayer a constant in our lives instead of reserving it for special occasions or times of need, we awaken the parts of us that are asleep or are constantly preoccupied with our physical, material world. One of my favorite quotes is "Don't tell God that you have a big problem, tell your problem that you have a big God." When we pray insistently, we put ourselves in the mindset of grace and flow in our daily lives because we stay connected.

Do you suggest that I write down my prayers?

Absolutely! Keeping a journal by your bed in which you write down your daily prayers, whether they are one sentence or long paragraphs, is so powerful and can be very soothing to your mind and heart. Writing down your prayers opens the channels to seeing new possibilities and receiving solutions, and it enables you to feel your connection to the spirit within.

Acknowledgments

Thank you to my agent, Bill Gladstone, for believing in this book and for consistently nudging me and asking me for a proposal so that we could make this book happen. So grateful to Donna Loffredo, my brilliant editor at Penguin Random House/ Harmony Books, for adding her magical touches to the manuscript. And to Katherine Leak who assisted with every detail and kept us moving forward. Julia Ireland was a godsend to me. She helped me put the proposal together and added so much value to the final stages of the manuscript with her impeccable gift for structuring a book. A big thank-you to Jahmie Hilecher, the perfect sounding board, who was there at the most challenging time during the pandemic, taking down all my thoughts and wholeheartedly supporting me as the book was birthed. And to my wonderful assistant, Lauren Aiello, who has been a great source of support in all of my work.

I have been blessed with the most loving and supportive circle of friends, who give me valuable feedback and always inspire me to keep going. Jan Shepherd, Faith Bethelard, Heide Banks, Joan Witkowski, Michael Hayes, Melba Ahonte, Shelley Reid, Elaine Lipworth, Lucia Ruehlemann, John Tarnoff, and Dyan Hasper-Johnson. Along with so many friends from the Thrive Global team, who are a great support to me—Danny Shea, Joey Hubbard, Marina Khidekel, Rebecca Muller, Mallory Stratton, and Kasia Laskowski.

And, of course, to my source of endless love and joy: my sister, Arianna, my beloved nieces, Isabella and Christina, and the new member of our family, Christina's husband, Paul Needham. Their love and presence in my life are heaven on earth for me.

My heart is full and grateful.

Also by **AGAPI STASSINOPOULOS**

Available wherever books are sold